How to ROAR:
Pet Loss Grief Recovery

By Robin Jean Brown

How to ROAR: Pet Loss Grief Recovery
by Robin Jean Brown

ISBN 1-4116-5653-9

Disclaimer

All material provided in this book is for informational or educational purposes only. The author of this book is a layperson who researched and wrote about pet loss after experiencing it herself. Therefore, no content is intended to be a substitute for professional advice, diagnosis, treatment, therapy, or counseling. Consult your doctor, therapist, psychologist, or psychiatrist regarding the applicability of any opinions or recommendations with respect to your symptoms.

Praise for *How to Roar*

Robin, when I lost my dog after 11 wonderful years, I was devastated. I felt all alone without my beloved companion. When I tried talking to people, they would laugh and tell me it's just a dog. After reading your guide and doing the exercises, I'm feeling tremendously better than before. I'm still grieving, but I'm thankful that now I have a helpful resource to comfort me.

Jennifer T.
Anderson, SC

I wanted to say you did a great job on this book. You have done a wonderful job and I think it will help so many people during this time.

Great Job,
Michelle

I've owned many pets from the age of 5. They've left me one by one. And I've never known how to truly overcome the grief until I read your book. Next time, I'll be prepared for such loss!

Epi A.
Darwin, Australia

I had the opportunity to read this book a week before we had to help our Bear pass on. It brought me so much comfort and hope that words will never adequately express my gratitude. Truly a treasure and one I will recommend to friends and family who are also experiencing the grief of losing a beloved furbaby.

Thank you so much, Robin.

Hollie Jackson

Having experienced the loss of a pet very important to me, I found many helpful ideas in Robin Jean Brown's Pet Loss Guide. As grief over the loss of a pet is not necessarily validated by the society in which we live, it is refreshing to read a book that deals respectfully with such grief. The text is easy-to-understand, and the journaling exercises provide ample opportunity for the self-expression necessary to the healing process. I think this book would benefit anyone dealing with the loss of an animal, regardless of species.

Deana S.,
Athens, GA

At first I was skeptical that a book could help me work through the death of my dog. But once I started reading it seriously, and using the journaling questions, I learned a lot about myself. I would recommend this book to anyone who has lost a pet and doesn't know what to do next.

Alexandra S.
Michigan

I'm thankful that Robin wrote this. Please read How to ROAR if you're hurting from your pet's death. It will help you through the pain.

Janice Stevens

After I lost my darling cat, I was desperately searching for a book to ease my pain. My son got me Robin's ebook and printed it out for me. I cried when I was reading and filling out the questions, but it comforted me and healed me. I was comforted to know that Robin Jean Brown went through the same pain that I went through. We were both so close to our pets. They were soulmates.

Paula Matthews

Table of Contents

1. How to Use This Guide

I understand that the loss of a pet can be a very difficult situation. I hope this book will help you to gain a healthy perspective so that you can better cope with the painful and normal grief that results from such loss.

For maximum results, use the book with your favorite pencil or pen. The pages of this text will not only explain the grieving process to you, but they also operate as your journal to collect your thoughts and ROAR through pet loss.

I explain my concept of ROAR at the end of this book, but here is what the acronym stands for:

R = ***Respect your loss and grief***
O = ***Own your reality***
A = ***Affirm yourself***
R = ***Reclaim your life***

You'll also notice that I don't talk about myself much in this book; that is intentional. You see, this book is about **you**. Only you can truly understand the emotions that you're going through.

But believe me; I have suffered through terrible grief, very recently, as I'll shortly explain. Writing this book was part of my own healing process, and in this book, you will be writing your own story, by answering the questions at the end of each section.

The questions are meant to guide you through the process, but don't feel bound by them. Many thoughts will come to mind while you are grieving and these worksheets need only be a starting point. Good luck on your journey!

Please note that even though you may be suffering the loss of a different type of animal than those used in this book (mostly dogs and cats), the elements of the loss and the coping are the same. It doesn't matter whether you've lost a rabbit, a rat, a horse or any of the many types of animals that people keep as pets.

2. Introduction – My Story

Like a lot of people, I've had pets my whole life. In elementary school, I had gerbils, a cat and a bulldog. In middle school, I had a pet frog, a guinea pig and two dogs that I got from the animal shelter.

And also like a lot of people, I've had to deal with the tragedy of pets dying my whole life. Until recently, probably the hardest loss I've experienced was when I was little and our bulldog ran away.

When our family dog Clyde "ran away," I was very sad and I felt an emptiness in my 9-year old life, blaming myself for what I thought had happened. My parents later told me that Clyde had actually been run over by a car. I survived, and as the years went on, we got more pets and everything was fine.

Flash forward to today. My beautiful, noble, intelligent Border collie mix, Andy, was my life. It was hard moving to new places because of my job, and leaving my friends and family behind. But even though it was hard I always had Andy by my side. For a while he was my best friend and the only "person" I could talk to every day. He was always with me and totally loyal no matter what.

In the fall of 2004 Andy started feeling really sick and run down. The top of his head looked and felt strangely sunken in. I took him to the vet and in January 2005 Andy was diagnosed with inoperable brain cancer. The news was shocking, but I was determined to give Andy the greatest life any dog could ever have during all of his remaining days.

His decline was steady. His vision was decreasing with each passing day, and by February he was blind. Then he started going to the bathroom in the house, which was so unlike him because he was always the best-behaved boy, and he would never think to do something like that.

When Andy died in April 2005, it was different than the other times I had experienced the loss of a pet. People told me that my loss would get better with time, but it didn't.

Day after day the feelings continued. I was deeply, overwhelmingly distraught – so much so that I would just sit on my couch and not move all day. My whole body ached, like I had the flu. I wouldn't eat. I didn't want to live anymore without my baby boy. (And that was SCARY because I've never lost the will to live before.)

I had reached bottom emotionally, and I felt so completely worn out.

I didn't know what to do. No one understood what I was feeling. I tried to ask for advice, and none of it worked. People would tell me to "get over it." But that was easier said than done.

I looked around for books on the subject of pet loss and grieving and found they weren't readily available. So I kept investigating. Once I had done some research, I realized that this would be the perfect opportunity for me to write a book (which I'd always wanted to do). It used to be that I wanted to write the great American novel, but now, since I couldn't stop grieving over the death of my baby boy, what better subject to write about than the grieving process? And what better tribute to my beloved pet? I was motivated and inspired.

The writing process helped me more than I ever imagined it could. It is because of my own experience that I believe this book to be an important resource. You see, this is not just a book that you read passively. It offers a step-by-step approach for you to work – not to "get over it" (since we can never "get over it") – but to at least *understand* your grief, move towards the acceptance stage, and eventually become happy again (which is what our deceased pets would want).

I truly believed that researching and writing this book would be good therapy for me, and it was! I immersed myself in this project. I exhausted all research possibilities, devoured every book I could find on the subject of dealing with grief, and talked to everyone I knew who'd faced the grief of pet loss. When I was finished writing, I was able to think happy thoughts again. I could remember Andy and smile rather than cry.

I hope that my book and the questions I ask you to think about will help you as much as they have helped me.

Journaling Questions: Who Are You?

Remembering who you are is important during the grieving period. Focusing on your life and your future will help you to get through this difficult time. And this is where the journaling exercises begin. Get your pencil or pen and fill in the following:

Name: _____

Self-Description:_____

_____

_____

_____

_____

_____

_____

Drawing or Photo – can be of yourself, you and your pet, or anything that makes you smile:

How has your life been made better by animals?

_____

_____

_____

_____

_____

_____

_____

Compile a list of all of the pets you've ever had a relationship with. Be sure to include descriptions and/or pictures as well as your age when you had them.

_____

_____

_____

_____

_____

_____

_____

_____

_____

How does your pet timeline define your life? How does it make you feel?

_____

_____

_____

_____

_____

_____

_____

When were your best times?

_____

_____

_____

_____

_____

_____

_____

_____

When were your most challenging moments?

_____

_____

_____

_____

_____

_____

_____

_____

_____

3. In the Beginning...There Were Pets

"Animals are such agreeable friends – they ask no questions, they pass no criticisms."

-George Eliot

I've loved all my pets very deeply. I hope this doesn't sound crazy, but I sometimes love animals more than a lot of people I encounter. Unlike people, your pets love you unconditionally, they never pass judgment on you, and they're never intentionally mean to you.

As a pet owner yourself, you know that today, people keep more than just dogs and cats around the house. While these are probably the most common types of domesticated animals, they're certainly not the only ones. The following section includes a brief history of the different types of pets people keep nowadays.

Birds

People first kept birds as pets nearly 4,000 years ago. Pet birds were depicted in Egyptian hieroglyphics, and parrots in particular were highly respected by the ancient Greeks and Romans. Birds have even been good enough for royalty: Christopher Columbus gave Queen Isabella of Spain a pair of parrots in 1493.

Cats

Cats have been pets for the past 5,000 years and were first domesticated in the Valley of the Nile. The ancient Egyptians at first enlisted cats in the battle against rats, but soon the cats became beloved by those who took care of them. The Pharaoh wanted all of the cats for himself to protect his vast quantities of grains, but his people would not give them up. He declared cats demigods and they became the ultimate property of the Pharaoh, though the people could still care for them.

Many people today would say that their housecats believe themselves to be demigods still. Their graceful independence is what helps them remain one of the most popular pets today.

Chinchillas

These funny little creatures look like balls of fur and love to bathe in the dust. Interestingly, they are virtually hypoallergenic and make great pets for those with allergies to other animals.

Dogs

Historically, people first used dogs to help track game and to participate in war. Ancient Egyptians spiritually associated dogs with death and the afterlife. During the early Greek and then Roman empires, dogs started to assume the role of pet and began to appear in artistic endeavors.

In the Middle Ages, purebred dogs were the prized possessions of kings. Even the Church widely approved of dogs. People started bringing their dogs to church services and using the animals as their foot warmers.

Today our beloved canines are still known for their fidelity and are generally seen everywhere with their human companions.

Ferrets

Ferrets were first used in rodent prevention and are known to have been domesticated since the year 4 B.C. Domesticated ferrets can still chase and catch prey, but have little ability to survive through the hunt. Ferrets are lively and energetic pets that are always fun when at play.

Gerbils

Gerbils are jumping desert rats that hail from Africa, Asia and parts of Eastern Europe. Scientists first brought them to North America for research purposes in 1954, but since that time gerbils have found their place in homes around the world. These curious pets aren't cuddly, but they do like to be held. You'll love watching them investigate their environments.

Goldfish

While the precise origin of the goldfish as a pet is unknown, it has been suggested through ancient Chinese artifacts that goldfish have been a part of Chinese households since approximately AD 800, initially in outdoor ponds. Goldfish were brought inside at the end of the nineteenth century. These popular pets provide as much companionship as their furry and feathered counterparts.

Guinea Pigs

Guinea pigs descended from wild rodents in the highlands of northern South America. These cute pets have been bred for more than 400 years and first became popular as pets in 16th century Europe.

Hamsters

Zoologist George Waterhouse first discovered the hamster in 1839. In 1930, another breed of hamster was discovered in Syria. First used in labs, hamsters found their way to the pet market during the 1970s. Since that time they have become one of the most popular pets because they are friendly and easy to maintain.

Horses

Humans first domesticated horses around 3000 BC in the Ukraine and Central Russia, much later than other farm animals and even dogs. Though we love them as pets, horses were once considered a significant food source. They were often used as work animals, but once people learned how to tame horses, they began to appreciate horses for much more than food and work. We now see horses as companions and care for them as we do for smaller house pets.

Pigs

Once kept exclusively as livestock, pot-bellied pigs increasingly have become fashionable pets. Contrary to the stereotypical hog living in a barn filled with mud, pet pigs are clean, intelligent, and highly emotional animals. The bond between person and pig can be deep.

Rabbits

The rabbit was first seen as a source of food and was commonly brought to islands with this goal in mind. Rabbits are highly appreciated by Native American culture in a variety of ways. For example, Algonquins believed that the "Great Hare" repopulated the world with his offspring after a destructive flood and the Iroquois devoted a special dance to the rabbit. Rabbits are fun and social pets that will play nonstop. They are devoted and cuddly companions to be sure.

Rats

It might sound strange if you're unfamiliar with these wonderful animals, but since the nineteenth century rats have been bred and ultimately domesticated. (Today's pet rats are no more similar to their wild ancestors than dogs and cats are to theirs.) There are even shows that are devoted to rats. These clean animals make for interesting pets with great personalities, and those who choose them as companions become very attached to them.

Journaling Questions: What Makes a Good Pet?

What qualities do you look for in an animal companion?

_____

_____

_____

_____

_____

What is the most important quality in a pet? Why?

_____

_____

_____

_____

_____

What are the benefits of having an animal companion?

_____

_____

_____

_____

_____

_____

_____

_____

What are the challenges involved with having an animal companion?

_____

_____

_____

_____

_____

_____

_____

How do you know which animal is right for you?

_____

_____

_____

_____

_____

_____

_____

Who was your first pet? Describe this pet.

_____

_____

_____

_____

_____

_____

_____

_____

_____

Journaling Questions: Who Is a Pet Person?

What does it mean to be an animal lover?

_____

_____

_____

_____

_____

What does it mean to YOU to be an animal lover?

_____

_____

_____

_____

_____

_____

_____

What qualities are necessary to be an excellent animal lover?

_____

_____

_____

_____

_____

4. The Rainbow Bridge

Whenever I've been faced with pet loss or pet death, turning to poetry has always helped me grieve. Interestingly, I've found that poetry has helped many people I've talked to who have also lost a pet. Perhaps poetry will also help you cope with the pain of pet loss. I'd like to share some of my favorites with you.

The Rainbow Bridge Story
Author unknown

Just this side of Heaven is a place called Rainbow Bridge. When an animal dies that has been especially close to someone here, that pet goes to Rainbow Bridge. There are meadows and hills for all our special friends so they can run and play together. There is plenty of food, water and sunshine, and our friends are warm and comfortable.

All the animals who had been ill or old are restored to health and vigor; those who were hurt or maimed are made whole and strong again, just as we remember them in our dreams of days gone by. The animals are happy and content, except for one small thing; they each miss someone very special to them who had to be left behind. They all run and play together, but the day comes when one suddenly stops and looks into the distance. His bright eyes are intent; his eager body quivers. Suddenly he begins to run from the group, flying over the green grass, his legs carrying him faster and faster.

You have been spotted, and when you and your special friend finally meet, you cling to each other in joyous reunion, never to be parted again. The happy kisses rain upon your face; your hands again caress the beloved head and you look once more into the trusting eyes of your pet, so long gone from your life but never absent from your heart.

Then you cross Rainbow Bridge together...

The Rainbow Bridge Poem
Author unknown

By the edge of the woods, at the foot of a hill,
Is a lush, green meadow where time stands still.
Where the friends of man and woman do run,
Where their time on earth is over and done.

For here, between this world and the next,
Is a place where each beloved creature finds rest.
On this golden land, they wait and they play,
Till the Rainbow Bridge they cross over one day.

No more do they suffer, in pain or in sadness,
For here they are whole, their lives filled with gladness.
Their limbs are restored, their health renewed,
Their bodies have healed, with strength imbued.

They romp through the grass, without even a care,
Until one day they start, and sniff at the air.
All ears prick forward, eyes dart front and back,
Then all of a sudden, one breaks from the pack.

For just at that instant, their eyes have met;
Together again, both person and pet.
So they run to each other, these friends from long past,
The time of their parting is over at last.

The sadness they felt while they were apart,
Has turned into joy once more in each heart.
They embrace with a love that will last forever,
And then side by side, they cross over......together.

Skeeter
by Forrest Phelps-Cook
From Reflections of the Heart

No flags were flown at half mast
when my little baby died;
no limousine to carry her home
no crowds of mourners cried.

But the world for me stopped turning,
my heart is filled with pain

my tears could fill an ocean
I want to see her again.

I want to say I'm sorry
to feel her lick my face,
I want to hold her close to me
and always keep her safe.

I wonder how to end this hurt,
to ease my troubled soul,
I wonder how I can go on
without her I'm not whole.

And so I pray to God above
to take care of my child,
say thanks that she was here
if only for a while.

And I will love another,
though she'll always be a part
of everything that's good and kind,
she will always have my heart.

I know that she is happy,
She is running in fields of gold,
and though I know she misses me
she'll someday be mine to hold.

So sleep my little baby,
your spirit now is free,
sleep my little baby,
you're still a part of me.

(Used with permission of Forrest Phelps-Cook.)

Journaling Questions: Where They Came From

After the loss of a pet it can comfort you to think about the when's and how's of your relationship. Complete the following worksheet to jumpstart this process.

Your pet's name: _____

Where did _____'s name come from?

_____

_____

_____

_____

When did you find your pet?

_____

_____

_____

How did you come to be with _____?

_____

_____

_____

_____

_____

_____

Why did you choose _____ above all others?

_____

_____

_____

_____

_____

_____

What did you love about _____ immediately? Why?

_____

_____

_____

_____

What did you learn to love about _____? How did you do it?

_____

_____

_____

_____

_____

_____

_____

What are your favorite memories of _____?

_____

_____

_____

_____

_____

_____

_____

_____

_____

_____

_____

_____

_____

_____

_____

_____

_____

_____

_____

Describe _____. Draw a picture or attach a photo as well.

How did _____ make your life better?

When was _____ the greatest comfort to you?

_____

_____

_____

_____

_____

What was _____'s favorite thing to do? Place to sleep? Toy?

_____

_____

_____

_____

_____

_____

If _____ could have talked, what would he or she have said?

_____

_____

_____

_____

_____

5. Why Do We Have Pets?

"Until one has loved an animal, a part of one's soul remains unawakened."

- Anatole France

The answer to the above question is different for each one of us. Animals offer companionship, unconditional love, and loyalty. In return they ask for very little. Our pets want food, shelter, health, and our attention. And we are always ready to comply.

Healing Pets

The health benefits of having an animal companion are numerous and they have been documented. Beyond the unconditional love and affection our pets provide, the medical benefits associated with pet ownership include:

- ✓ Decreased blood pressure
- ✓ Decreased cholesterol levels
- ✓ Increased physical activity
- ✓ Decreased likelihood of depression
- ✓ Improved and consistent general health
- ✓ Relief from stress
- ✓ Promotion of social interaction
- ✓ Fewer trips to the doctor
- ✓ Satisfaction of the need for touch
- ✓ Increased happiness and emotional strength
- ✓ Constancy when faced with a fatal or degenerative disease

Teaching Pets

It's also true that we learn from our pets every day. Pets teach us about responsibility and love and help us to interact with others. Children especially benefit from pets because they learn how to care for another being. As children, many of us were responsible for the feeding and care of a pet, and this experience helped us become responsible and caring adults.

One of the best lessons that can be taught by a pet is that of happiness. Unless they sense danger or feel pain, you won't often see an unhappy pet. The wag of a dog's tail or a cat's purr reminds us that what is important in life is to be happy.

Helping Pets

Animals can be trained to assist those who have disabilities. Specially trained animals can be the eyes, ears and hands of the people they assist. Without the help of these loyal companions, many of those with disabilities would have difficulty maintaining their independence.

Beyond the role of official aids, there are many animals that participate in programs that help the elderly, the sick and even the incarcerated. The presence of animals can reduce stress levels and help people to love and show interest in another life no matter what their circumstances are. Many "working" pets make frequent trips to hospitals, jails and nursing homes to visit those people in need of some extra unconditional TLC.

Comforting Pets

A happy dog, cat or gerbil can serve as motivation for getting up and moving around even if you're tired or feeling under the weather.

Pets and the Elderly

Pets can be of particular comfort to the elderly for psychological, medical, and social reasons. The health benefits of pet companionship are clear. Socially speaking, many pets often provide the company that is so often craved by the elderly. When children or grandchildren live far away, a loyal pet can fill the void.

Journaling Questions: Animals In the World

Thinking about the presence of animals in the world can provide a certain level of comfort. Respond openly to the following questions.

Where do you encounter animals every day?

_____

_____

_____

_____

_____

_____

_____

_____

_____

What is your favorite fiction or non-fiction animal story? What makes it your favorite?

_____

_____

_____

_____

_____

_____

_____

_____

_____

What films, documentaries or television shows do you watch that include or even focus on animals? What do you like about these shows?

_____

_____

_____

_____

_____

_____

_____

_____

What type of book, film or TV show would you like to see about animals?

_____

_____

_____

_____

_____

_____

_____

_____

_____

_____

How are animals depicted in the news?

_____

_____

_____

_____

_____

_____

_____

What do you know about animal rescue organizations? How could these be better promoted?

_____

_____

_____

_____

_____

_____

_____

_____

Where and how are animals missing from the public eye?

_____

_____

_____

_____

_____

_____

_____

6. How Deep Is Your Love?

"It often happens that a man is more humanely related to a cat or dog than to any human being."

-Henry David Thoreau

The relationships between humans and animals are complex and unique. The level of bonding and attachment varies widely amongst pet owners and is not easily generalized. This being said, there are some trends that situate pet owners and their companion animals along a scale of attachment. Look at the scale below to determine how you would define the relationship with your pet.

1	2	3	4	5
Disinterest/ Cruelty	Bare Needs Attention	Traditional Care	Family Member	Intimate Bond

Sadly, there are pet owners whose relationship with their pets falls into the first two categories, but they are discussions for another book. For our purposes, we will be concerned with categories three, four and five. Take a close look at the above scale again. You may find yourself in any one or all of these categories. Remember, this is not meant to be a strict classification, but merely a guideline.

If you are reading this book because you're looking for advice on helping a friend deal with the death of a pet, you may find it helpful to refer to the sections on grief and memorials. It's okay for you to not share their feelings of grief as long as you can respect the fact that they have experienced a significant loss.

It may be difficult to see the loss of a pet as a significant factor in a person's life, but there are many people who are intimately connected to their animals, as you will see below. Consider the following definitions of bonding and the accompanying stories to see what others have done in times of grief and pain.

Intimate Bond

This level of attachment most often is reserved for those who live with a companion service animal or for those who see their pet as a life partner or a child. Those who have a service animal see the animal as an extension of him or herself, and the loss that is felt when such a pet dies is considerable.

Quite often, people who might otherwise not relate well to other humans relate intimately to animals. It seems to be the people who have experienced mistreatment or trauma at the hands of other humans who feel most comfortable basking in the unconditional love of an animal. It's also common for a pet to be a replacement for people who may be absent from everyday life or a friend to those who may be otherwise isolated from contact with the world at large.

At this level, the grieving process likely will be long and complex and not unlike the experience of those who suffer the loss of a close human family member such as a parent or child. Others who do not understand the degree of your grief over the loss of your pet may further complicate your grief. In fact, it is common for people who are not bonded at all with animals to see grief for a pet as illegitimate.

An Intimate Bond Example:

Mary and her Rhodesian Ridgeback Max were inseparable. Wherever Mary went the dog was soon to follow. After the death of her husband, Max became Mary's sole daily companion, and she saw him as her life partner. Vacations were never taken unless Max could come. She even hesitated to visit Europe with her friends because she would be unable to bring Max. Max was treated as the man of the house, the king of the castle. He had the best foods, the best vitamins and the best care of any animal alive.

One day as they went for their morning walk, Mary noticed that Max was limping. She immediately called the vet and made a rush appointment for that afternoon.

The results were not what Mary wanted to hear. The vet discovered that Max had bone cancer and that it had already spread to other parts of his body, specifically to his lungs. There was very little to do except keep him comfortable in his last days.

Mary spent a great deal of money to medicate Max and to keep him with her as long as possible. They continued to take their walks and to lounge on the porch in the afternoons for nearly three more months before Max passed away. One morning Mary woke up and got ready for her morning outing with Max, but he had died peacefully in his bed at her bedside overnight.

When she first learned of Max's condition, Mary found a reputable pet cemetery in her area and contacted them for advice, as difficult as it was for her to think about at the time. She said her initial goodbye to Max and phoned the cemetery. They were to come and get the body to prepare it for burial.

Mary called her best friend, who immediately came over, and the two of them spent the afternoon contacting those who would come to the burial service the next day. Later that evening, just before bed, Mary talked to Max and started writing in this workbook journal that she had printed from her computer.

This was the beginning of her grieving process. The service was of great comfort to Mary and it was what began to give her the closure she needed to survive.

Little by little Mary began to find happiness in her life and to remember fondly her beloved Max. Though she initially couldn't imagine connecting to another pet, she did miss having an animal in her life. She started volunteering at a local no-kill animal shelter and even became a foster pet sponsor. One day she walked into the shelter and the most jubilant puppy jumped on her, wagging its tail. She knew then that she had found her new partner. Gracie came home with Mary the next day and from then on happily lived by her side.

Family Member

The people who see their pets as quite literally members of the family form deep and emotional attachments to their animals. Their pets are considered to be the "babies" of the family and quite often no expense is spared to improve their quality of life—be it for medical treatments or a deluxe pet bed.

If you see yourself in this category, the lengths to which people go to care for their animals may not surprise you. It's likely that you research the best type of food and exercise for your pet and that you spare no expense when it comes to your baby's happiness. Your pets live in your laps and on your furniture, and anywhere they wish. They want for nothing and are often spoiled.

This level of attachment will result in a deeper level of grief than experienced by the Traditional Care families. It will be important to more fully explore the grieving process and perhaps even spend more active time in this process. You may hold a more formal service, choose a burial over a cremation, and elect to do something in memory of your pet whether you buy a memorial item or participate in a fundraising activity that relates to animals.

A Family Member Example:

Ellen and her daughters, Kristin and Lauren, loved their lively Lhasa Apso/Shih Tzu mix, Charlie, from the day he came home to them. He slept in bed with one of the girls at night and lounged on the couches in the daytime. His favorite activities were sleeping in someone's lap or getting a new toy. No dog had as many toys as Charlie, and he especially loved Christmas when he was sure to get a pile of presents wrapped just for him.

Charlie had always been a happy, well-behaved dog who never damaged the house or suffered from aggression issues. Then one day the family started noticing that he was having accidents in the house and becoming quite a grouch. He even nipped at their neighbor's kid! The family tried to ignore Charlie's behaviors for as long as possible, but the mess became too much. They took him to the vet who explained that he was aging and beginning to suffer a form of dementia. There was nothing that could be done to alleviate the situation.

The family brought Charlie home and tried to act as if everything was normal, but they all knew that Charlie wasn't their Charlie anymore. In the end, they took him back to the vet who peacefully euthanized him and cremated the body. The family kept Charlie's cremains in a special engraved box and thought of him often. Eventually they buried the box along with his favorite toy.

At Christmastime the family decided to give a donation to the local animal shelter in lieu of their normal gift buying. One day they may get another pet of their own, but for the time being, they like where they are.

Traditional Care

This level of attachment is the most common type of relationship. The animal is a member of the household, but is not viewed as being as important as the human members of the family. Often there is a lack of strong emotional attachment from the humans in the relationship. However, these pet owners care genuinely for their pets and maintain them responsibly. Grief is experienced at the Traditional Care level of attachment, but it usually is briefer than for the previously discussed two levels.

Nonetheless, it is still important to respect the grief process. Consider hosting a simple family memorial service and packing up the pet's belongings immediately. Also, change any schedule you follow that centers on the pet. For example, if you typically get up in the morning and walk the dog, you might want to consider another activity such as exercise, yoga or reading the newspaper. Consider the following example to see if this is similar to your human-pet relationship.

A Traditional Care Example:

Sandy and Jack lived with a loveable black cat named Sally. Sally had always led a comfortable, fun life in the large backyard with her own custom-made shelter that Jack had built for her out of wood.

Sally was especially happy when Sandy and Jack spent time outside with her on the weekends and evenings, but she would have loved to spend more time with them. Sally was by no means neglected, but she was more attached to her people than her people were to her. Sandy and Jack loved her, but they only spent time with her when it was convenient for them.

One day they noticed that she was having trouble breathing and decided to make an appointment with the veterinarian. They soon learned that fluid was building in her lungs due to a failing heart. For a few months they gave her medication that seemed to help a little, but in the end her quality of life was rapidly declining.

Finally, they made the decision to euthanize her. Jack was particularly affected by the death of Sally because he was the one who attended to her the most. Initially his grief was intense, but after a few weeks the couple started talking about a new pet.

The stories of Sally, Charlie, and Max may be similar to your own or they may be completely different. But the point is, you don't need to have a story like theirs (or the same animal as theirs) to learn from them. Each situation is different and each bond is different. In fact, you could even have multiple pets and a different bond with each of them.

What's important when thinking about the bond with your pet is to really examine your relationship and what it means to you. This understanding will help when it comes time to move on. Saying goodbye is a difficult task and each of the pet owners in the stories above needed to do it in their own way. And so do you. The next journaling section will help you better understand the bond you have with your pet.

Journaling Questions: Defining Your Relationship

This next journaling session is an opportunity to describe the specific nature of your relationship with your pet using short paragraphs and lists. Take your time so you can express yourself creatively and honestly.

What did _____ (pet's name) mean to you? Why?

_____

_____

_____

_____

_____

_____

_____

_____

_____

_____

_____

What was his or her most important role in your life?

_____

_____

_____

_____

_____

_____

How did _____ operate within your family? How did other family members see him or her? (Remember, not all families are traditional in nature. Think about your non-traditional family network as well.)

_____

_____

_____

_____

_____

_____

_____

_____

_____

_____

How did you show your love for your pet?

_____

_____

_____

_____

_____

_____

_____

_____

How did your pet show his or her love for you?

_____

_____

_____

_____

_____

_____

_____

_____

What did you provide for each other? Provide specific lists. Do you find any of these things with other companions? What conclusions can you draw from this?

_____

_____

_____

_____

_____

_____

_____

_____

_____

_____

_____

7. How Do I Know I'm Grieving?

What does it look and feel like to grieve? Though it is different for everyone (and some of these symptoms are indeed, polar opposites), you may experience any or all of the following while you grieve:

Crying

Confusion

Fatigue

Withdrawal

Anxiety

Emotional Inconsistency

Loneliness

Physical Pain

Inability to Sleep

Excessive Sleeping

Feeling Like You Have to Be In Motion

Real-Seeming Dreams of Your Pet

Numbness

Feeling Empty

Shortness of Breath

Tightness in Throat, Chest

Despair

Apathy

Vulnerability

Feeling Abandoned

Inability to Make Decisions

Desire to Make Others Comfortable

Hyperactivity

Lack of Energy

Guilt

Lack of Appetite

Feeling Overwhelmed

Irritability

Difficulty Concentrating

Inability to Function Day to Day

Impulsivity

Weight Loss

Weight Gain

Aimlessness

Searching for Something

Forgetfulness

Lack of Interest

Lack of Initiative

Dependence

Over-Sensitivity

Journaling Questions: Research

After the loss of a pet, it may help to learn more about who your pet really was. Do some research on your pet's breed (or for mixed breeds, one of the breeds they descend from) using the following pages to guide you. This will also be a helpful exercise to complete when and if you choose to look for a new animal companion.

Animal Type: _____

What is the historical origin of the breed?

_____

_____

_____

_____

_____

Where were these animals originally found? How did they come to be found in other parts of the world?

_____

_____

_____

_____

_____

_____

Did these animals serve any other purpose? List these other purposes.

_____

_____

_____

_____

_____

What sort of variety is found in the breed?

_____

_____

_____

_____

_____

What type of personality does the animal have? What type of human companion best suits it?

_____

_____

_____

_____

_____

_____

_____

How well does this animal interact with other animals? How can you introduce this animal to other animals successfully?

_____

_____

_____

_____

_____

_____

_____

What is the best way to acquire this type of animal?

_____

_____

_____

Do you know of any rescue organizations that are devoted to this animal? Where?

_____

_____

_____

_____

What accessories are required to create a happy home for this animal?

_____

_____

_____

_____

_____

What is the best way to train this animal? List any particular areas that need special training and attention.

_____

_____

_____

_____

_____

_____

_____

What food options are best for this animal? List any particular dietary issues.

_____

_____

_____

_____

_____

_____

_____

_____

What are the average lifespan, weight and size of this animal?

_____

_____

_____

_____

_____

What is the best way to exercise the animal?

_____

_____

_____

_____

_____

_____

List any specific medical conditions associated with the breed and any general health issues owners should be aware of. What vaccinations do they need?

_____

_____

_____

_____

_____

_____

_____

_____

How does this animal need to be groomed?

_____

_____

_____

_____

Why does this animal make a good pet?

_____

_____

_____

_____

_____

_____

_____

8. Grief 101

"Grief is love not wanted to let go."

- Earl A. Grollman

Dr. Elisabeth Kubler-Ross defined a five-stage grief process in her groundbreaking book, *On Death and Dying*. These stages include:

Denial

Bargaining

Anger

Sadness

Acceptance

These stages present a framework for grief that can help people work through and better understand their pain. The grieving process is an individual one and as such these stages vary in length and intensity for each person. For example, denial could be fleeting, but anger could overwhelm the sufferer.

Likewise, these stages do not necessarily occur in the same order for each person and some stages could repeat. It is important for those grieving to listen to themselves and acknowledge their own experience of the grief process.

Denial

For weeks after Andy died, sometimes I would forget he was gone. Then suddenly I'd remember and break down crying. I even called out his name one time when I was working on this book, even though I knew he wouldn't come.

Denial is your subconscious mind's method of self-defense. Quite simply, because the thoughts and feelings you'd have could be so painful, your mind refuses to acknowledge reality. When it does, you find yourself crying at random times.

When we're aware of something horrible, we instinctively want to believe that it's not true. This self-protective stage helps to insulate us from the pain. While in this emotional state we want to continue as if nothing has happened, to forget about the pain, and to ignore reality. This denial can even take on extreme forms such as not telling anyone of the death, shutting yourself off from even thinking about your lost pet, or continuing as if your animal companion is still living. (For example, you may continue to purchase items for the deceased or return home frequently to let the dog out.)

If you find yourself exhibiting these types of behaviors, don't feel like there is something wrong with you. Denial is a normal way to handle a loss. It's crucial to get past this stage, but it should be done according to your schedule, not that of those around you.

Action Plan for Conquering Denial

Honor your pet with a commemorative act.
This can be anything from a simple mention of your pet each day, to a formal service or memorial item. For more ideas, consider the options listed in the Alternative Memorials section of this book.

Keep your pet with you.
This does not mean visiting the taxidermist! Keep a picture of your pet with you, and maybe one of his or her possessions like a toy or collar. But you don't need a physical item to keep your pet with you. Just keeping your pet present in your mind can help.

Have patience.
Give yourself the time you need to work through your grief. This may not happen as quickly as you'd like, but in time, you will make it through your grief.

Talk to people.
Talking to friends, family, grief counselors, grief support groups, or just a man on the street will help you to move past denial. Talking about the loss can help to make it more real for you.

Cry.
I promise that you're okay and will eventually get through this grieving experience. I have cried every day for months after the deaths of my pets. Let your tears flow freely and for as long as it takes. Your pet was a huge part of your life, and his or her death cannot help but affect you. Imagine that grief is like a raging river. In order to get to the other side, you must swim through it. And if you avoid swimming through, you'll never get to other side.

Bargaining

When a loved one is dying, many people try to "bargain" with God or their Higher Power of choice. This usually consists of a series of negotiations: "If you let my loved one live, then I will be a better person, donate to charity, never yell again, etc." I certainly did my share of bargaining when I was rushing my cat Layla to the vet. I would have promised *anything* to have her survive.

We bargain as a way to feel as if we have control over an uncontrollable situation. It is clear that there is an element of denial within bargaining. We also bargain with the dying pet in the form of statements such as: "If you recover, I will never scold you again," or "I'll get you all the toys and great food you could ever want and make you the happiest animal in the world."

Making deals with a higher power or with our pets does not result in the desired tangible change of the situation, but it does help us to look outward and begin to connect with someone else over our grief. The danger is that these bargains may also lead to anger when the desired outcome is not realized. However, this is all a part of the grieving process.

As I just mentioned, I struggled with bargaining when my Siamese cat, Layla, died. She enriched my life for a precious short time. My baby girl was only 2 years old when she collapsed in my hallway. I sprinted to her to see what was wrong and discovered she wasn't breathing!

In the car rushing to the vet, I prayed and prayed as hard as I could. I pleaded for my God to let Layla survive, and if not, to at least let her death be peaceful.

It was anything but. I'll spare you (and myself) from giving the horrific details, but basically everything that could have gone wrong, did. The vets even botched Layla's euthanasia so when she died, she was alone and in pain.

When that happened, I wasn't just crying, I was wailing in agony. My God had double-crossed me and abandoned me. He had caused Layla undeserved suffering, from the point when she collapsed in my hallway all the way until her awful death. I felt completely helpless and flew into the worst rage of my entire life.

The lesson I learned was that bargaining causes more pain. Why? Because you can never count on getting what you bargained for and because bargaining results in feelings of bitterness.

Action Plan for Dealing the Bargains Away

<u>Try it.</u>
The bargains you are trying to make with yourself, with a Higher Power, and with your pet are ultimately NOT going to work. You can promise the moon, but the medical reality will be the same.

Nonetheless, it may help you to make these deals as a part of your grief process. As the stages are all tied together, this is clearly a reversion back to denial. You can only know that the bargains are fraudulent if you see it for yourself.

<u>Accept that bargains are meaningless.</u>
Once you've realized that the bargains won't change the situation, accept this truth and move on.

<u>Remind yourself how you've enriched each other's lives.</u>
Your pet is blessed to have had you as its human companion because you've got a shining heart and radiate an abundance of love. And you've been blessed to have your animal companion enrich your life with the unconditional love and the happiness that he or she gave you.

Anger

When my kitty, Layla, died, I was riddled with anger. I didn't understand what I had done to deserve to have such pain inflicted in my life. I wondered what my cat had done to deserve her pain. She was just an innocent little cat. All I wanted was to be able to say goodbye to her and to have her pass away in peace. But no! She had the worst, most painful death. I also raged at the vets for botching her euthanasia and causing her a miserable, sad, painful death. I felt so helpless and impotent and I wanted to lash out at everyone.

Anger, as a stage of the grieving process, is the emotional outburst that most often occurs after denial. The anger can be directed at yourself, other caregivers, friends or family, a higher power, and even towards the deceased themselves.

Being angry with yourself often becomes a massive attack of guilt where you begin to play the destructive "what if?" game with yourself. "If only I hadn't left the door open, she wouldn't have run into the street and gotten run over." "If only I had brought him to the veterinarian earlier, he could have been treated." A friend of mine was horribly angry with herself for leaving her canary's room open, which allowed her cat to attack and kill it. As her friend, it was scary to see how guilty her self-directed anger had made her feel.

In many cases, feeling guilty seals the pain of loss inside you and causes you to remain alone with your pain, for the very long term. On the other hand, being angry with others helps you to distract yourself from the loss (as was my case), which is why it is a psychological self-defense mechanism. Finally, in the rare case when you direct your anger at the deceased, it can help to assuage your feelings of guilt as it takes the blame away from you.

Grief is a complex process where your emotions become muddled. You may experience all of these versions of anger as time goes by. While anger is normal and healthy, it is important to work through it so that you can move onto other stages of grief.

My anger got better and then went away when I focused on the present moment rather than looking back at painful memories of the recent past. You see, right now, Layla is totally free of any pain or sickness. I believe she is in a better place now at the Rainbow Bridge, romping through the meadows without a care. She'll be happy there until that wonderful day comes when I meet her again.

Action Plan for Shutting Anger Out

Embrace your emotions.
Feelings are never wrong. You have a right to feel angry. What you need to do however, is to understand *why* you are feeling so angry. Understanding will be easier if you write down your case for why you are angry. Get out a piece of paper and write "I feel angry at _____ because of _____, _____, and _____."

Embrace logic.
Emotional responses such as anger cloud our rational and logical perspectives, and suddenly the highly improbable becomes the most reasonable explanation at that given time. Slow down and think calmly about why you feel angry. Who or what are you feeling angry about and why are you responding in this way? What are you accomplishing by feeling so angry? Cold logic can shake you out of your emotional torment.

Exercise.
Keeping yourself active is a great way to get your frustrations out and at the same time maintain a healthful lifestyle. Go for a walk or run. Sign up for boxing lessons. Do whatever it is that you enjoy doing. Exercise can clear the mind and body of that which ails it.

Allow yourself a release.
Scream into a pillow or punch a sack of flour! Do something to help get the anger out. A healthy release of emotion can help you to express the emotion appropriately. Becoming angry and physically violent with others should be avoided, however.

Find the truth.
Beyond being logical, find the truth. If your pet was ill, talk to the vet about the illness or research it on your own. Don't let yourself get bogged down with guilt and your own opinions on the situation. Take the initiative to learn about the reality of the situation because it will help you to move on.

Visualize your pet's new life.
Re-read the Rainbow Bridge poem. Be joyful that your pet didn't need to suffer another moment and instead is in a happy place right now. Think about how wonderful it will be when you are reunited with your pet in the future.

Sadness

This stage is what most people understand grief to be. Extreme sadness and sorrow are to be expected when dealing with the death of a loved pet, and it may be difficult to function as you normally would or to interact with others.

Sorrow manifests itself in both physical and psychological ways. Physically a griever may find it difficult to eat or sleep, may gain or lose weight, may experience restlessness or fatigue, and may even feel aches and pains. Psychologically it may become difficult to concentrate; emotions may run high and change from moment to moment. Other common symptoms include feelings of guilt or worthlessness, disinterest in life, frequent feelings of depression and thoughts of death or even suicide.

Also know that of the stages, this is the one you'll most likely experience more than once. You may feel fine after a few weeks, but then feel a certain pang around special times of the year that you spent with your pet. Fear and anxiety may be high during this stage, and emotional numbness and shock are not uncommon.

It's important during this time to avoid isolating yourself from the world. Remaining connected to friends, family, and other caregivers will help you to live through your pain.

During the sadness stage it's helpful to talk to others about your pain so that you can begin to deal with the reality of the loss. Reaching out to friends, professionals, and Internet or book resources will help you to begin the healing process. If you feel that your sadness is only increasing you should seek help immediately. There are many caring professionals who can help you through this time.

Down With Depression – The Action Plan

Learn the symptoms.
Know what to expect. This is not to say that there is a normal way to feel sad, but it does mean that the loss of a loved one affects each person differently. Someone

who has never experienced deep sadness might not understand what the griever is feeling.

Try to find the good.
It's difficult to think happy thoughts when you're feeling extreme sadness, but it's this positive thinking that will get you through the tough times. Try to find at least one good thing in your day and focus on that. Soon, you'll have trouble NOT finding a happy moment.

Talk, talk, talk.
This may be the single most important thing you can do to help yourself at any stage of the grief process. Having a good listener or someone to give their two cents can make the difference between a long painful process and a quick recovery.

Stay active.
Keep your normal lifestyle in place. Don't give up jogging for naps or hiking for television. Keeping active can also help you to avoid isolation and maintain your health.

Acceptance

The final stage of the grieving process is acceptance. At this point it's possible for you to accept that your companion has died.

During this stage you can start to focus on the relationship at its best. You still may experience sadness, anger, or guilt at your loss – but you can recover from these times faster. Plus, you're now able to look forward rather than backward.

It would be a mistake to see acceptance of a loss as the end of the grieving process, because acceptance is not an ending; it is a new beginning. Acceptance does not mean that you no longer think of your beloved pet. Instead it means that you have reframed the way in which you think about his or her death. In the early stages of the grieving process you are bogged down with emotion. Upon arrival at the acceptance stage, you can acknowledge the loss and you should be able to logically reflect upon the current situation.

With a focus on the present and a fond remembrance of the past, you can once again find happiness.

Action Plan for Acing Acceptance

Bring animals back into your world.
It may be too soon right now for you to consider getting a new animal companion, but eventually you could slowly bring animals back into your life by volunteering to walk the animals housed at your local shelter.

Am I Finished Grieving?

As I've said, the grieving process is often long and is always complex. It's normal and not unusual or crazy for you to feel that way. And remember, these are only guidelines to what you may experience. There is no set pattern or length of time for each stage. Right now, just know that you will make it through the hurt and pain and find joy again. You brought a pet into your home to enhance your life (and your pet's life) in a positive way. You were your pet's world, and your pet would want you to be happy again and not to mourn his or her passing forever.

Journaling Questions: The Stages of Grief

Hopefully you've learned more about the five stages of grief: denial, anger, bargaining, sadness, and acceptance. Now, use these pages to work through your thoughts and emotions during each of these stages.

Denial

What are you denying?

_____

_____

_____

_____

_____

_____

_____

How are you rationalizing the denial?

_____

_____

_____

_____

_____

_____

How is the rationalization faulty?

_____

_____

_____

_____

_____

_____

_____

_____

_____

_____

Why are you rationalizing?

_____

_____

_____

_____

_____

_____

_____

_____

_____

_____

_____

Anger

Make a list of all of the people and things that you're angry at and explain why you've chosen to be angry at these particular people or things. Be specific.

1_____

_____

_____

2_____

_____

_____

3_____

_____

_____

4 _____

_____

_____

5 _____

_____

_____

6 _____

_____

_____

7 _____

_____

_____

8 _____

_____

_____

9 _____

_____

_____

10 _____

_____

_____

Now that you've made a list, rank the angry items beginning with the one you've chosen to feel the most anger about and ending with the least.

1 _____

2 _____

3 _____

4 _____

5 _____

6 _____

7 _____

8 _____

9 _____

10 _____

Now, think about the two things that you feel most angry about. Write about what you could do to get rid of the anger. What is something that can make you smile when you're feeling this anger?

1 _____

_____

_____

_____

_____

_____

_____

_____

_____

2_____

_____

_____

_____

_____

_____

_____

How can you use your anger for something positive?

_____

_____

_____

_____

_____

_____

_____

_____

_____

Bargaining

What are the terms of the bargains you are making? Be specific.

1 _____

_____

_____

_____

_____

_____

_____

_____

_____

_____

_____

2 _____

_____

_____

_____

_____

_____

_____

_____

_____

3 _____

4 _____

_____

_____

_____

_____

_____

Which of these bargains would you most like to see realized? Why?

_____

_____

_____

_____

_____

_____

_____

_____

_____

_____

Why won't these bargains work?

_____

_____

_____

_____

_____

_____

_____

_____

_____

What else could you do instead of bargaining that would result in a positive outcome?

_____

_____

_____

_____

_____

_____

_____

_____

_____

_____

_____

Sadness

List the symptoms of your sadness, both physical and psychological.

_____

_____

_____

_____

_____

_____

_____

When do you feel sad? Is there a specific time that you always feel sad?

_____

_____

_____

_____

_____

_____

_____

_____

_____

What do you do when you feel sad?

_____

_____

_____

_____

_____

_____

_____

_____

What could you do to feel happy? What makes you happy?

_____

_____

_____

_____

_____

_____

_____

_____

_____

_____

Acceptance

When did you begin to accept the reality of your loss?

_____

_____

_____

_____

_____

_____

_____

_____

What helped you to accept your situation?

_____

_____

_____

_____

_____

_____

_____

_____

_____

What does it mean to accept the loss?

_____

_____

_____

_____

_____

_____

_____

_____

_____

_____

_____

_____

9. I'm Grieving, What Can I Do?

"It is better to learn early of the inevitable depths, for then sorrow and death can take their proper place in life, and one is not afraid. "

-Pearl S. Buck

It's only natural to grieve the loss of your pet. You and other family members likely will go through this process, and each one of you will experience it differently. While there is no right or wrong way to grieve, there are ways to get through it without endangering your health. Here are some valuable words of advice to keep in mind as you progress through the grieving process.

1. *Take care of yourself.*
    Taking care of yourself is your number one priority. Whether this means taking a short vacation, ordering meals out, taking a nap, going for a walk, or throwing a party, you should be doing what feels best for you. Be sure that you are eating and sleeping properly and that you aren't isolating yourself from the world. Wallowing in guilt and pain will not help you in the long run even if it seems like your only option in the present. Talk to a friend or to a professional. It could help!

2. *Acknowledge your feelings.*
    Accept your feelings as they occur without trying to stifle them. Don't feel guilty about anything that you feel. Know that your emotions are valid and move forward. Talk to friends, family, or even professionals if you need to get an outsider's perspective, but don't look to others to define your feelings.

3   *Expect to feel the loss physically.*
    Don't be surprised if you experience your grief in a physical way. You may lose your appetite, have trouble sleeping, feel ill or experience other physical symptoms. Pay attention to your body! You want to remain healthy.

4. *Exercise.*
    After I lost Andy, I started going to the gym religiously, pouring my heart into the treadmill and rowing machine. Being alone with my thoughts, yet still surroun-

ded by a comforting crowd of people helped me to clarify my thoughts. I went from feeling blah before going to feeling tremendous after every workout. Not a fan of exercise? Just try something new to get you going. There are great classes to take and friends to be with. Go for a walk -- whether it's at a park, zoo, mall or sports field. Go to a personal trainer or sign up at a gym. Go jogging outside and enjoy nature. Just find something to do to keep your body moving!

5. *Eat healthfully and regularly.*
You might not be hungry OR you may be hungry for all of the wrong things. Keeping healthy is important and eating a balanced diet is a good way to do it. Explore organic foods and try new recipes. Learn to eat well at restaurants! Cook for friends or your significant other.

6. *Rest when you need it!*
It's easy to run yourself ragged when you want to avoid dealing with pain. Don't do it! Exhaustion leads to illness, which can lead to further stress and depression. Stay active, but know that it's okay to spend the evening with a good book or with your favorite television vice too.

7. *Cry if you want to.*
Don't suppress your sadness and fears. You don't need to be brave for anyone. It's healthy to cry and get the emotions out as they come to you. Cry with someone you love or cry alone, but don't be afraid to do it. Remember, you don't need anyone's approval!

8. *LAUGH!*
Life should be enjoyed! Have fun and don't feel guilty for it. The healthy expression of happiness will give you strength.

9. *Don't go looking for stress.*
Sure, some stress is difficult to avoid, but you know how to make stress for yourself. Try not to do this. You can leave the dishes until tomorrow, make that phone call next week, and take on a new project at work some other time. Don't become anxiety-ridden over the small things.

10. *Abolish guilt.*
It will be normal for you to feel some guilt during the grieving process. Whether you feel that you could have done more, or you're uncomfortable about your own growing happiness, guilt will be lurking. While it is natural for you to feel this way, remember that you did all that you could for your animal companion and that you deserve to live happily. Saying no to guilt means saying yes to you (and your pet, since he or she would have wanted you to be happy).

11. *Establish a variable routine and follow it.*
This does not mean that you should become a robot, but it does mean that you should fill your day with a variety of things you like to do AND that you can do in

an organized manner. When you're grieving it helps to keep a schedule, but don't overdo it. One way to establish a routine is to take a few moments each morning to decide three goals for the day. In the evening, take a moment to reflect on what you've accomplished. Keeping a journal can help with this effort, even if it's just to record what you've done each day and how it makes you feel when you meet (or don't meet) your goals.

12. *Don't hide from the world.*
It may be easy to isolate yourself to avoid emotional scenes, but keeping to yourself can have a downside. Spending too much time living inside your head can make it more difficult to get through the grief process. It helps to get some input from the outside and communicating with others will make you feel good too. Make an effort to interact with people outside of your household at least once a day.

13. *But take that time alone when you need it.*
Get familiar with your own limits. Putting yourself on an exaggerated social and work roller coaster will not make you forget the difficult period you are going through. Organize your life so that you can comfortably spend time alone or with others.

14. *Avoid destructive behaviors such as drug or alcohol abuse.*
On paper, this sounds like a fairly obvious tip. But when the bottle's in front of you, it's easy to think that you can escape the pain by taking a drink. The reality is, however, that by doing so, you're only postponing the inevitable. Doing long-term damage to your health is never a good option, regardless of the situation. Work through the pain. Don't try to suppress it through artificial means.

15. *Participate in activities you enjoy.*
Do you have a hobby? If not, now is the time to seek one out. Go to sports events, wine tastings, cooking courses, comic book conventions – your options are practically endless. Think about your interests and find a way to become active. If you enjoy long walks, make it a point to go on one weekly! Do what you can to be a happy member of the world.

16. *Bring fun and positive change into your life.*
Try something new. Take an adventure. Celebrate all the amazing things that surround you and appreciate life. Your pet brought you happiness and would want you to continue to live joyfully.

17. *Ask for help when you want it.*
It's okay to ask for help. Sometimes people don't know how to help you when you're grieving, but they would love for you to tell them. Whether it's running an errand or having dinner together, your loved ones would be thrilled to help out. Don't feel guilty about asking since they're probably waiting for your call.

18.   *Help someone in need.*
Volunteer to help humans or animals. Seeing that others are working through difficulties too may help you feel a sense of community. In helping others, you are helping yourself.

19.   *Don't become grief.*
You may be grieving, but you are not only grief. Remember all the great things in your life and hold on to them. Certainly you'll have days when remembering happy times will be difficult, but don't create a life of misery for yourself.

20.   *Schedule time for grieving.*
Scheduling your grief may sound a bit insensitive, but it could help. Set aside a specific amount of time during your day to think about your loss and your grief. TIME your grieving session and try not to exceed the limits that you make for yourself. Realize that you aren't forgetting your pet if you're not suffering every minute of the day. Your pet brought you happiness and would not want you to suffer excessively. Be reasonable.

21.   *Be patient with yourself.*
You may feel out of control and not like yourself, and these feelings will be frustrating. Be patient! Give yourself the same chance you would extend to others. Let yourself feel these feelings and soon you'll return to your comfortable state.

22.   *Recognize that a bad day is not the end of the world.*
Learn from Scarlett O'Hara and remember that tomorrow is another day. Look to the future and do what you can do to celebrate life. Dwelling in the past will keep you there.

23.   *Stop asking "why?" and ask "what will I do next?"*
There may not be an answer to the question why, but you can decide what to do next. Moving forward while remembering fondly your beloved pet is a good way to get through the grieving process. A "poor me" attitude is a slippery slope to further depression.

24.   *Realize that you will survive.*
Tell yourself this until you believe it. Make it a daily affirmation and it will be true. It will be difficult to do this at first, but with each day you will have renewed hope and interest in life.

25.   *Make decisions carefully.*
Don't jump to make decisions, but don't agonize for weeks over simple daily activities. Trust yourself, assess the situation, and decide. Don't be regretful.

26.   *Say goodbye.*
Say goodbye to the pain and sorrowful memories, not to your cherished past
your pet. Hold on to the good times and make them a part of your present li
Close the door on tragedy and choose a happy life track.

27.   *LIVE!*
This is the most important tool to remember. Focus on life and your grief will
dissipate into joy.

10. Pre-Loss Grieving

For many of you, the grieving process will actually start BEFORE your animal baby dies. This is referred to as "pre-loss grieving" and it's normal. This happened to me when I lost Andy. When I found out on that horrible January day that my baby was definitely going to die, I became a basket case. For days I couldn't stop crying. I missed that entire week of work.

The vet did say that chemotherapy was an option for Andy, and that there would be about a 5% chance that the cancer would go into remission. But he also stated that the cancer had spread into Andy's bones making recovery even less likely.

Of course, we always know intellectually that our pet is going to die someday. Even when our pet first enters our lives – just a frisky little kitten or puppy – we know intellectually that our furbaby will definitely die too soon. Maybe it'll be in just a couple of years, as with a pet rat, or maybe it'll be in 10 years, but that horrible day will come as surely as the sun sets at night.

In her book *Coping With Sorrow On the Loss of Your Pet*, Moira Anderson Allen wrote that "pre-loss bereavement begins when you realize not just intellectually, but emotionally, that you are going to lose your pet." Furthermore, as Allen points out, you feel like there's no way to get over the grief because the loss hasn't actually happened yet!

During pre-loss grieving, you might find yourself going through all the stages of grief, particularly the bargaining stage. In my case, I'd say, "I'll spend any amount of money Andy, to keep you alive. I'll do whatever it takes!"

I spent days like that until suddenly I came to a realization that set my heart at peace. The underlying cause of my pre-loss bereavement, I realized, was living in the future. I was grieving for something that WOULD come – but hadn't yet.

All I had, I realized, was the present moment. And Andy was still alive in the present moment. You see, we only live in the here and now. And if NOW Andy was alive and with me, why shouldn't I spoil him like crazy and enjoy every precious moment I had with him?

I showered Andy with all the love I had. I would constantly tell him how much I loved him. I took as many pictures as I could, filling albums with his images. I filled video tapes with movies of him. Even though my time with him was short, I was thankful that I could make him the happiest dog that ever lived.

I gave him all his favorite foods! He loved chicken and especially cheese. I wrote him letters telling him all about why I loved him so much. I spent every present moment I had experiencing him – imprinting my brain with his smells, his sounds, and the way he felt when I cuddled with him. I let him sleep on my bed with me for the first time ever.

Looking back on this pre-grieving stage, I realized that it was my happiest time ever. I say this even though tears are streaming down my face as I write. It was the happiest time of my life simply because I had just that: TIME. I was given time with Andy and I was going to enjoy every present moment I had with him.

So my advice to you in dealing with your pre-loss grief is to enjoy every moment you have with your baby and to follow your heart. Give your pet pain medication to keep him or her from suffering. And at the end, when the time comes for you to give your pet the greatest act of love, remember that you'll be releasing your pet from pain and sending him or her to the wonderful Rainbow Bridge.

11. The "Do's" of Helping a Loved One Grieve

What if you're not the one grieving the loss of a pet? What if the person who is grieving is a friend or a loved one? Would you know the best ways you could offer support to this person? Here are some useful tips on how you can help another person work through the grieving process.

1. *Respect that the death of a pet means no less than the death of a human.*

    It may be difficult for non-pet owners or pet owners with different types of relationships with their pets to understand the extent of the loss. It's crucial to respect the griever even if the perspective of the caregiver differs.

2. *Immediately contact those who are grieving to let them know you are there.*

    Make a concerted effort to contact your grieving friend. When struggling through the grief process, it's all too easy to isolate oneself from the rest of the world, even from trusted friends and loved ones. So you need to be the one to reach out to those who hurt. Your extra effort will definitely be noticed and appreciated.

3. *Admit your own feelings of helplessness.*

    Grief is difficult even for those serving as the support system. You may not know what to say. ADMIT THIS. Using these exact words say, "I don't know what to say." It's much better to admit feelings of awkwardness and ask the griever what he or she needs than to remain silent. Silence breeds guilt for you and does nothing to help the person in true need.

4. *Volunteer to stay with your friend or invite your friend to your home.*

    It may be difficult for someone who has experienced the loss of a domestic animal to remain at home alone. It may be comforting to have a guest or it might even be comforting to leave home entirely for a night or two. Either way, this would be a good time to reminisce about the deceased and to pamper the person in need. Take the opportunity to create a special time with a special dinner or activity that is tailored to the likes of the griever.

5.   *LISTEN!*

The single greatest thing that you can do for someone who has experienced a loss is to listen once that person feels talkative again. Talking about the deceased pet and/or about feeling guilty or angry are common topics. But the conversation can be about anything. The point is that being there to listen to whatever your friend or loved one has to say will help immeasurably. Ask open-ended questions and allow the griever to direct the discussion. If the one grieving feels the need to repeat the story a number of times, that's okay. Just LISTEN!

6.   *Provide silent comfort.*

As important as listening can be, it is equally important to offer silent support. Just being in the same place as the griever may be a comfort. When you visit, bring a book. After a bit of conversation, your friend may just want to sit quietly with you. Believe it or not, this is a great way to help.

7.   *Educate yourself about grief specific to your loved one's situation.*

The death of a pet is a very specific type of loss. You should spend some time investigating the situation. Take time to find out more about that type of animal that died and about the grief process. You should not necessarily report all that you've learned to the griever, but you may find that some of your newfound knowledge will help. Many great books are available and you'll find a wealth of information on the Internet.

8.   *Keep in touch even after the initial period of shock.*

It's easy to remember that your friend is in need during the moment of the crisis but don't forget to check in later. The grief process is not quickly completed and it's helpful when people remember that the griever is still experiencing grief long after the death of the pet. Just a simple phone call or brief email will do the trick nicely.

9.   *Write a note.*

Have you noticed that people don't send mail anymore? Sending a thoughtful "I'm thinking of you" card will speak volumes to your friend and will be a welcome surprise. You don't need to write a novel. Just let the person know that he or she is always in your thoughts. Do this frequently, especially if you don't live near your friend or loved one.

10.   *Let the griever know it's okay to express his or her emotions with you.*

People experiencing grief may feel timid about expressing their emotions even with the closest of friends and loved ones. Let the person know that you are there unconditionally. Make it clear that whether the person feels a need to cry, scream, laugh, or otherwise express an emotion, you're there to listen and lend a shoulder. This is especially comforting because those experiencing grief are prone to isolation.

11. *Offer practical and specific help.*

It is not helpful to say, "Let me know if you need anything." This puts pressure on the griever to ask for help when he or she may feel anxious about asking for it. It's likely that you know your friend well and know what could help. Offering to do a specific task helps your friend and doesn't allow for guilty feelings to develop. Examples of helpful tasks might be to make a meal or to go grocery shopping. If your friend volunteers in some capacity, but feels like taking a day off, you could offer to go instead. You can always offer to do tasks around the house or even to help with tasks. Accompanying your friend on errands might just be the best kind of assistance you can provide. Be creative and trust your heart. Good intentions won't lead you astray.

12. *Talk about the griever's lost companion and share your memories of the pet.*

Don't be afraid to talk about the deceased. Share your stories and feelings about the pet. In this time it's important for those grieving to hear how much their companion was loved. Listen to the wonderful memories and ask questions. Show interest in what was near and dear to your friend.

13. *Encourage them to grieve in their own way.*

Let your friend or loved one know that there is not a right way or a wrong way to grieve. Acknowledge the pain and allow the other person to do whatever it is that he or she needs to do to make it through the grief process. Just listen and remind the one grieving to follow his or her heart.

14. *Provide resources that may help.*

In learning about grief yourself, you can provide your friend with resources that you have found. Books, websites, and phone numbers can help to answer questions about grieving. There are excellent support services available to those grieving for a pet and it may help your friend if YOU take the initiative to find out some of this information. Don't force your findings on the person, but make the information available if he or she seems open to it.

15. *Help with a memorial service if one is planned.*

Keep your personal beliefs of this event to yourself. It does not matter whether or not you would plan a memorial service for a deceased pet. What is important is that you assist in the process if the person you're comforting plans a memorial.

Offer to handle the invitations or to run errands. Help out in whatever way you can and never belittle the process.

12. The "Don'ts" of Helping a Loved One Grieve

As stated previously, there is no right or wrong way to grieve. The best advice is to allow the person to experience it in his or her own way, as long the person is not endangering his or her mental or physical health. It's natural to feel the need to offer advice, however try to keep the following in mind as you interact with the one who is grieving.

1. *Don't tell someone how to grieve.*

    There is no single way to grieve, so each individual must decide how to deal with it. The role of a supporter means one of helpful assistance. Imposing a potentially inappropriate standard upon someone in pain is counterproductive. Be a listener and a friend, and you'll provide what a griever needs above all else.

2. *Don't avoid the griever because you're uncomfortable.*

    Death is difficult for EVERYONE. Admit it to yourself and to your loved one and move on to the next step. Learn about the grieving process and death and work to become more comfortable. It's much better to let a griever know how you are feeling and that you don't know what to say. This honesty will be welcomed and is preferable to avoidance. Avoidance isolates the griever when one of the things he or she needs most is to be with a support system.

3. *Don't try to make the griever forget by keeping busy.*

    You'll never succeed in making a griever forget the current reality. It's not necessary to forget, either. Acknowledging and experiencing personal grief is the only way to get through it. Attempting to keep a griever's mind off of the death makes it seem as though YOU want to forget about it and may make the person grieving rethink your help and motivation.

4.   *Don't compare grief.*

Recounting your own story of grief or that of another does not do much to help a griever. No experience of grief is the same, so comparisons actually reduce the importance of the individual's grief. This also takes the focus away from the griever. It can make him or her feel as if it's time to stop grieving and get on with life, which can actually make the grieving experience worse. Reminding loved ones that they are not alone is a good idea, but implying that the grief is insignificant is not.

5.   *Don't make the grief about you.*

Helping someone through grief is a wonderful thing, but you're not doing it to demonstrate your magnificence. Don't become the martyr of someone else's difficult situation. You may feel that your work isn't being recognized, but it is. Another time you may be in need, and you will want your friend to help you in an unconditional way too. Try to remember to treat a person who is grieving as you would want to be treated in a similar circumstance.

6.   *Don't overwhelm with stories about your life and your wonderful LIVING pet.*

This is not the time to describe how your dog has learned a new trick or is in superior health. This is not to say that you shouldn't acknowledge the existence of living animals, but don't make it the focus of conversation. Use common sense during your conversations with the griever and discuss things that he or she wants to talk about. Don't let the person fall into the miserable "why me" trap.

7.   *Don't try to explain another person's loss.*

Understand that explaining the logical reason for the pet's death or turning to an explanation rooted in the will of a Higher Power is not comforting. Surely your loved one knows the reality of the loss, but it's not that easy for those who grieve to use logic during a time of shock. Just offer support and understanding without judgment.

8.   *Don't be impatient.*

At times it might be difficult to hear that story about Fluffy for the 100th time in three days but this is when you need to listen most. Showing impatience and frustration will only hurt the griever who may already feel strange about expressing so much emotion. The last thing that should be done is to make the griever feel guilty about his or her feelings and needs. Be a friend. You may already know the story, but listen again.

u know how the person feels.

#1 error people make when speaking with someone who is
grief. You'll never know how another person feels even if you've lost
In saying that you know how the person feels, you minimize the
individuality of their situation and relationship with the pet. A comment like this
will not encourage your friend to look to you for help.

10. *Don't tell the person when or how to stop grieving.*

Every grieving process is different. There is no specific timeframe that must be
followed. People need to work through pain on their own schedule. Respect the
grieving process as an individual one and allow your friend to make his or her
own decisions. Be supportive without being bossy.

13. Helping You Help Me

When you've suffered the loss of a pet, or any loss for that matter, it's common for those who surround you to not know what to say or do. While concerning yourself with how others may be acting or feeling shouldn't be your primary concern, there are ways you can help make life easier for yourself and your supporters.

1. *Ask for help.*

    Ask directly for help. Don't hint, and don't use secret code or try ESP. Just come right out and ask. Better yet, ask for something specific. If you need someone to run an errand, ask for it. If you want someone to come over and keep you company, ASK. Do you see where I'm going with this? Most people are just waiting for you to say something and hoping you will soon. And, as usual, this goes without saying: DON'T FEEL GUILTY FOR ASKING!

2. *Forgive anyone who accidentally puts a foot in his or her mouth.*

    Understand that your loved ones are trying. They don't want to be insensitive, but they just don't know what you're feeling and never will be able to. If they say or do something awkward, let it go because it was most likely inadvertent.

3. *Ask for honesty.*

    Your loved ones may not know what to do or say. Let them know that it's okay for them to be in the dark. You are probably not feeling much more certain about your situation than they are. Let them know that you don't expect them to know what to do and that you'd like them to figure it out with you. They'll be grateful for your admission.

4. *Be honest.*

    Tell your friends and family how you're feeling. If they say something that could be hurtful, don't interpret it that way. They may not understand your experience of grief, and it is unlikely that they're trying to hurt you. Keeping the lines of communication open is better for all involved and will help you to experience grief with the support you need.

5.   *Express your feelings openly.*

Don't try to be brave for your friends. You need to let them see how you are feeling so that they can better help you. It's often difficult, but it's helpful to disclose your feelings to your social circle. Ask them to express their feelings too! Open discussion is one of the most helpful tools to use during the grieving process.

Journaling Questions: Getting the Help You Need

You've probably noticed that your loved ones don't always know what to say to you during your period of grief. Use this worksheet to brainstorm about the people that make up your support circle and how they can better help you.

Make a list of the people closest to you and describe how they most support you. Include people you may have met recently in the course of your grieving process.

Name: _____

_____

_____

_____

_____

Name: _____

_____

_____

_____

_____

Name: _____

_____

_____

_____

_____

Name: _____

_____

_____

_____

_____

Name: _____

_____

_____

_____

_____

Name: _____

_____

_____

_____

_____

Name: _____

_____

_____

_____

_____

Name: _____

_____

_____

_____

Now, compose a list of things you think you need in terms of grief support. This can include specifics like help with errands or childcare or finding established support groups. Also think about the type of emotional support you might need. Do you need a listener? Do you need someone to be your "logical" sounding board? List all that you can think of and remember that nothing is too great or too small.

1_____

_____

2_____

_____

3_____

_____

4_____

_____

5_____

_____

6 _____

_____

7 _____

_____

8 _____

_____

9 _____

_____

10 _____

_____

11 _____

_____

12 _____

_____

13 _____

_____

14 _____

_____

15 _____

_____

Now that you've written your two lists, try to match your supporters with the support you need. As you compile this list, be sure to write down why you feel a particular person can best help you with this particular need.

Name: _____

_____

_____

_____

_____

Name: _____

_____

_____

_____

_____

Name: _____

_____

_____

_____

_____

Name: _____

_____

_____

_____

_____

Name: _____

_____

_____

_____

_____

Name: _____

_____

_____

_____

_____

Name: _____

_____

_____

_____

_____

Name: _____

_____

_____

_____

_____

Name: _____

_____

_____

_____

Now that you've identified your needs and the people you feel are best able to help you meet your needs, consider talking to your supporters one-on-one. If in-person communication isn't possible, send a note to the person saying, "I appreciate your friendship." Then explain how you think he or she can help you in this difficult time.

14. Understanding Guilt

"Guilt is the very nerve of sorrow."

-Horace Bushnell

As pet owners, we take on a special responsibility to keep a living being alive and happy. We give these animals our unconditional love and we work selflessly for them.

Unfortunately, we naturally tend to be perfectionists when it comes to our pets, which means that if we neglected any little thing before the animal's death, we feel guilty over it.

What is guilt?

Merriam-Webster defines guilt as "feelings of culpability, especially for imagined offenses." *Imagined offenses.* When our pets are sick or dying, we think back to all the things we did "wrong" or to the times when we believe that we did not do enough. Ultimately, we convince ourselves that our action or inaction is what contributed to the current situation. These are our "imagined offenses," and these are what cause our guilt.

Guilt can manifest itself in a variety of ways:

✓ Feeling responsible for the death that has occurred.

✓ Feeling regret because you could have done more or made better decisions for your pet.

✓ Feeling ashamed because you had a moment of happiness.

✓ Feeling upset because you didn't say goodbye properly.

✓ Feeling shame because you weren't there.

Guilt typically takes a prominent place in the grieving process. We expect ourselves to be super-human, to be perfect, and that just isn't possible. Attempting to live up to idealized standards leads directly to feelings of guilt. This can easily be identified as "should-ing" yourself to death: "I should have done this; I should have done that." These "should-based" thoughts could go on forever, but nothing you did or did not do will ever change the circumstances you are in.

Why choose guilt?

1. *Feeling guilty will lead to forgiveness.*

    It's easy to think that the only way to purge the guilt is to receive forgiveness from an outside source – whether it's from our animal companion from beyond the grave, or from members of society who are judging our actions. But there's nothing to forgive, and if anything, you need to forgive yourself for creating such a guilt-saturated environment. You've done nothing wrong and you need to accept that.

2. *Guilt will alter the circumstance positively.*

    You may think that if you feel badly enough, things will change. Unfortunately this is faulty logic combined with denial. Your emotional state is affecting your ability to move on. Accepting that your guilt is preventing you from healing is an important step to take.

3. *People will respond positively when you express guilt.*

    You may think that others expect you to feel guilty and that if you do not act guilty then there's something wrong with you or that you are a bad person. These thoughts are created by you and only you. Outsiders are probably not concerned with how much guilt you feel, and even if they are, it should not affect your reality.

4. *You can avoid working on the present when you feel guilty and focused on the past.*

    It's easy to wallow in guilt. Sure, you don't feel great, but others pay attention to you AND you don't need to do anything to move past your current circumstances. Remaining in the depths of guilt is the ultimate in laziness because you are avoiding the present and reality.

5. *You can stay safe, emotionally speaking.*

    If you feel guilty you don't need to feel anything else. You can avoid the real reasons behind your pain. Turning yourself into a guilt automaton makes you one-dimensional.

What is guilt doing to me?

1. *Immobilizing*

    You freeze yourself for fear of saying, doing or being "wrong." You ignore your feelings and emotions and become completely inactive. Guilt can make you live as if you were in an emotional coma. You experience nothing good or bad from the outside world and become isolated even from those you love.

2. *Irrationalizing*

    You are no longer able to see the boundaries of reason and begin to falsely rationalize your situation. You may be unable to make new decisions, but you are able to obsessively analyze past decisions, especially those surrounding the loss of your pet.

3. *Over-sensitizing*

    You begin to see everything as a personal commentary on you. Things that people say and emails that you receive all become subject to over-analysis that, in your mind, attack you critically. You feel guilty about this even though the other people likely are not even thinking about you in that horrible way you perceive.

4. *Confusing*

    Your fear of making a mistake will confuse your thoughts. You'll suffer inability to make a decision because you'll be so wrapped up in weighing the consequences. This muddled thought process is not helped by your emotional (and now functional) immobility.

5. *Denying the self*

    You are slowly erasing yourself. Your concerns for others' opinions and for the possibility of making a poor decision do not allow you to respect yourself as a person. You mask your identity through the guilt you're drowning in. Everything about you is now reduced to your guilt – either as an expression or consequence of it.

6. *Pressurizing*

    You are taking on responsibility for everyone and everything. There is such a thing as being *too* conscientious, and this is the pressurizing effect of guilt. You ignore your own needs and do whatever it takes to attempt to make others happy. Though this may seem like a positive project, you are actually negatively motivated to be so "helpful."

What does guilt sound like?

Guilty thoughts are based in irrational beliefs that we have about ourselves. Irrational beliefs are messages that we send ourselves that immobilize us in guilt. These unfounded opinions are counterproductive and distract us from the work we need to do to move on. It's easy to get into the habit of using irrational beliefs and the resulting guilt as crutches when "handling" difficult circumstances. Though, the truth is, all that we are doing is postponing the inevitable confrontation with reality.

Here are some examples of irrational thoughts that feed our guilt about death:

- ✓ I don't deserve happiness.
- ✓ I can't survive this loss.
- ✓ I'm responsible for the pain the entire family is feeling.
- ✓ I shouldn't feel happiness when my pet just died.
- ✓ I shouldn't be so concerned about myself.
- ✓ I didn't do anything right.
- ✓ I should grieve in a way that others find appropriate.
- ✓ I shouldn't bother anyone with my problems; they don't care.
- ✓ There is something wrong with me; why else do I feel guilt?
- ✓ I caused this.

When you are weighted down by irrational beliefs and guilt it is difficult to pull yourself up, but there are some important benefits to proving our irrational beliefs to be false:

- ✓ We gain greater clarity about our current situation.
- ✓ We become more productive.
- ✓ We can take active steps to solve our problems.
- ✓ We mobilize emotionally and are able to feel good again.
- ✓ We are realistic about the present.
- ✓ We can plan what to do next.
- ✓ We can find ourselves again.
- ✓ We laugh, cry and yell.
- ✓ We are healthy.
- ✓ We rejoin the world and reintegrate ourselves socially.
- ✓ We begin to abolish our feelings of guilt.

Journaling Questions: Identifying Irrational Beliefs

A cornerstone of guilt is buying into an irrational belief surrounding your pet's death. You may feel that the death is your fault in some way, that you could have done more, or that you made a poor decision. Working past the irrational belief and finding the reality of the situation will help you banish guilt from your present.

What is your irrational and limiting belief?

_____

_____

_____

_____

How do you feel when you think this?

_____

_____

_____

_____

_____

_____

_____

_____

_____

_____

What evidence supports this belief?

_____

_____

_____

_____

_____

_____

_____

_____

What will happen if this belief is not true?

_____

_____

_____

_____

_____

_____

_____

_____

What belief, rooted in truth, could replace this belief? How?

_____

_____

_____

_____

_____

_____

_____

_____

How will this new belief change your outlook?

_____

_____

_____

_____

_____

_____

_____

Why have you been holding on to your irrational belief?

_____

_____

_____

_____

_____

_____

_____

_____

Imagine you could let go of your irrational belief. How would that feel?

_____

_____

_____

_____

_____

_____

_____

_____

15. Getting Rid of the Guilt

"Let other pens dwell on guilt and misery."

-Jane Austen

Conquering guilt is a major step in the grieving process and doing so can help you to live with your loss rather than being a slave to it. To help you, I suggest following the action plan outlined below. It will help you to get rid of the guilt you're feeling about the death of your beloved pet.

Step 1: Am I plagued by irrational beliefs?

You've already read about irrational beliefs and have seen the damage they can do and the role they play in constructing and maintaining a guilt-ridden environment. Ask yourself if you are "should-ing" yourself to death. Most likely, you are. You're probably telling yourself that you should have done more, you should have been around, you should have made a different decision, you should have done this, and you should have done that. These are the irrational beliefs that are fueling your guilt.

Step 2: What is this so-called belief?

Think about your should statements. What are they about? Write down all those that you say to yourself and then think about why you are talking to yourself in this way. Try to reduce the irrational belief down to one statement. An example could be: "I am responsible for my pet's death." A so-called belief such as this is very powerful especially when ingrained in someone who is experiencing grief.

Step 3: Is this rational? Of course not!

Now that you have identified your irrational belief, take it apart. Ask yourself how this can be true. Where do you see problems in the logic of the statement? Let's take for an example, "I am responsible for my pet's death." Did you physically cause the death of your pet? Did you indirectly cause the death through neglect? The answers to these questions are probably NO. If so, you have the power to undo the irrational belief and replace it with a rational belief.

(But what if you did cause the death of your animal through some neglectful behavior? Wallace Sife tackles this question in his book *The Loss of a Pet*. Suppose someone lets antifreeze spill in the garage, killing the cat that laps it up. Another person accidentally backs over their dog that was sleeping behind the rear wheel. Although we may indeed be responsible for the animal's death, we must learn to accept our ultimate helplessness. It's not possible for any human being to be vigilant 100% of the time, every moment of your life. You're not perfect. Nobody is.)

Step 4: I BELIEVE!

Now that you've discovered the irrational belief, it's time to instill a rational and healthy belief that will help you to grow and embrace life. You need to affirm that you deserve good things in your life and that you cannot be weighed down by the negative and false beliefs to which you have been subscribing.

Step 5: Where's the guilt?

You'll find that without the support of an irrational belief, it will be very difficult for you to exist guiltily, immobilized by fear and doubt. Though it's natural to feel guilty for a time, it is important not to dwell on it. Guilty denial of the reality of your situation prevents you from reaching your goal – to be happy and live a fulfilled life.

Step 6: Happy thoughts

Think about all of the good times that you spent with your pet. You might even want to write out a list for yourself. You aren't doing this to make yourself sad, you're doing it to embrace the great times you had with your pet. Your pet brought you happiness and it's better to cherish those times rather than focus on the pain of loss.

Step 7: Give yourself some credit

Remember all of the good times that your pet had. Then remember that your pet had these good times **because of you**. You loved your pet and you gave your pet a great life. All the way to the end you were generous and selfless. Were you perfect? No. But you loved your baby and brought great joy into his or her life.

Step 8: What's my GOAL?

Now that you've erased the guilt, you can get on with the business of living and loving. Respect your feelings and emotions without creating a dire place for yourself. There is a place for all of your emotions (both happy and sad), and part of your new goal can be to find balance in your emotional life.

Journaling Questions: Guilty Thoughts

It is hard not to feel guilty when you are grieving the loss of a pet. Use this worksheet to work through your guilty thoughts and reframe your perspective.

Are you responsible for your pet's death? Why? Why not?

_____

_____

_____

_____

_____

_____

_____

_____

Who is responsible? Is anyone responsible? Why? Why not?

_____

_____

_____

_____

_____

_____

_____

How have you made this situation worse for yourself?

_____

_____

_____

_____

_____

_____

_____

_____

_____

How guilty do you feel? What does your guilt look like?

_____

_____

_____

_____

_____

_____

_____

How does guilt make this problem worse?

_____

_____

_____

_____

_____

_____

_____

_____

What would it be like if you didn't feel guilty? How would it change the situation?

_____

_____

_____

_____

_____

_____

_____

16. When a Child's Pet Dies

"Music is best understood by children and animals."

- Igor Stravinsky

The death of a pet can be very traumatic for a child because a child often relates to an animal differently than adults do. Children often see their pets as their best friends, the ones they share secrets with. Dealing with the loss of a pet might be difficult for you as an adult, but it's very important that you monitor your child's behavior so you can help your child get through the grieving process as well. This may be the first time your child experiences death so it's important to give your child all the facts he or she needs to properly grieve.

Age Matters

The age of the child at the time of loss is significant and should be considered. The more you communicate with your children, the better they will be able to handle the loss and the better you will be able to help them.

✓ Children two years old and under will not understand death, but they will feel the anxiety that you are feeling. Provide reassurance and let them know that you are okay.

✓ Children older than two and less than seven will not fully understand the permanence of death. Be honest with them and encourage them to ask questions and talk about their pet.

✓ A child older than seven and younger than twelve will understand what death means and that it is permanent. Be sure to answer all questions and encourage your child to express his or her feelings.

✓ Older children may have trouble expressing their feelings of grief and loss. It is important that you let them know it is okay to be angry and sad.

How to help

1. *Let your child be part of the process.*

   If your pet falls ill and you know that death is imminent, do not hide this fact from your child. When you're discussing options such as hospice care or euthanasia, explain what this means to your child and let your child participate in the decision making process. When you don't explain what's happening to your family pet, your child can feel confused and left out.

2. *Talk to your child about death.*

   Explain what death means. Your child, depending on age and maturity level, may have a different idea of what this means. Use appropriate words like death, dying and died. Do not say that the pet has been put to sleep or has gone away. Children need to know that death is permanent. If you use euphemisms a child will wait for the animal's return and during this time may not be able to grieve. Answer your child's questions, but don't provide information that is not asked for. Children know what they want to know and anything else could be overwhelming. Be prepared to answer the same questions more than once.

3. *Show your grief in front of your child.*

   Expressing your emotions may be difficult, but it is important for your child to see that it's all right to be emotional. Tell your child how you're feeling and ask them what they're going though. Knowing that it's okay to cry or to be angry and sad can make a big difference. Children take their cues from the adults in their lives, and if you're repressing your grief, your children will do the same.

4. *Let your child grieve in the way he or she deems appropriate.*

   As with adults, it's important that you respect a child's expression of grief. Remember, everyone grieves differently, including children. Children may or may not want to talk about the pet's death. They may ask seemingly inappropriate questions or say that they hate their pet. These types of behaviors are simply part of their grieving process. An individual's grief does not follow a general timeframe which is why it's important to let your child work through the situation as he or she sees fit.

5. *Seek professional help and support when necessary.*

   As a parent you're probably very tuned in to your child and you will know if you need to seek outside help. Support groups are available for both parents and children and attending one to learn how to handle grief might be helpful for all family members. Another option is to contact a professional to ask how to best help your child. It cannot be stressed enough that each grieving process is different which is why it's so important to monitor your child's progress.

6.   *Hold a memorial service.*

Each family will operate differently, and so will each child. He or she might wish to have a funeral for the pet. It's important to respect the child's wishes even if you're not in favor of a memorial. Your child might want to remember the pet in other ways too, like making drawings and scrapbooks or planting a tree. These are great ways to not only commemorate a beloved pet but to also let a child actively grieve.

7.   *Inform the other people in your child's life of the loss.*

Talk to the other adults in your child's life (teachers, day care providers, neighbors, and family) to let them know what has happened. They can help to monitor your child and assist the child with grief. If your child's friends ask about the death of the pet be honest but be sure to also inform their parents of the situation.

8.   *Think carefully about getting a new pet.*

Generally speaking it is a good idea to give everyone the time they need to grieve before getting a new pet. Depending on the age of your child, it may be more or less difficult to accept a new pet immediately. You will want to consider getting an animal that is different from the deceased because it may be upsetting for you and your children to see what could be a "clone" of your beloved and deceased pet.

17. Quality of Life

"All animals except man know that the ultimate of life is to enjoy it."

- Samuel Butler

If your pet becomes ill, quality of life issues move to the forefront. Quality of life for humans and animals is not all that different when you examine the issues that make living most satisfying.

It's important that you focus on your pet's happiness when considering quality of life issues rather than on your own. It will be difficult to disregard the change in your quality of life that likely would occur if you were to lose your pet, but think about your pet. Observe your pet carefully, whether it is ill or elderly, and determine your pet's quality of life. I've outlined some behaviors to monitor.

Factors

1. *Awareness*
    Does your pet often seem disoriented or confused? Does your pet forget where his or her food is or what the command "sit" means? If yes, then these could be simple signs of aging or perhaps the loss of vision or hearing. If you can, offer comfort as your pet's confusion can often lead to fear. If the confusion degenerates to more serious dementia, for example, the animal forgets that he or she is house trained or the pet becomes aggressive, you'll need to think seriously about how this is contributing to your pet's quality of life.

2. *Happiness*
    The emotional state of your pet is quite subjective, but you likely have lived together for some time and if so, you probably are in tune to your pet's feelings. You need to be careful that you are actually seeing and not projecting what you'd like to see as far as your pet's demeanor is concerned. Be honest with yourself about your pet's behavior. Does your dog typically run to greet you, tail wagging? Does your cat purr when you walk into the room? If you start to see changes, it is

possible that he or she is in pain or discomfort and because of the pain, is no longer able to be happy.

3. *Appetite*

Has your pet stopped eating or become excessively picky? How much must you work to encourage your pet to eat? If your pet is not eating enough to sustain its body, he or she is on the path to slow starvation. It's time to consult your veterinarian. There may be supplements you can provide for your pet, and if so, you should. Your vet will be the best source of information on your pet's health.

4. *Mobility*

This is an obvious quality of life issue. When your pet begins to have trouble sitting or standing, and when walking becomes a laborious chore, there is a problem. Of course there are degrees of mobility. An occasional limp is not the same as hind legs that drag. Nevertheless, you should be vigilant in considering the life that your pet is leading. You must also take yourself into consideration. If you need to carry a 60-pound dog up and down flights of stairs, or you must clean up after a dog that can't stand up in time to make it outside, you need to consider your quality of life. An unhappy pet will ultimately make you unhappy as well.

5. *Incontinence*

Again, this is an obvious quality of life issue. An animal that is no longer able to relieve himself appropriately is not happy. It is part of the animal code to seek out appropriate areas to go to the bathroom. An animal that is not able to do this is not happy and could very well feel ashamed. Beyond the feelings of the animal, it becomes difficult for owners to constantly clean up after ill pets.

6. *Breathing*

If your pet is having difficulty breathing or is panting excessively, there could be fluid gathering in the lungs due to another condition. You will want to consult your veterinarian. If this is caused by simple allergies or some other treatable issues such as an infection or asthma, you can solve the problem with medication. If the situation is more serious, like cancer or heart failure, you need to consider the comfort of your pet. Labored breathing is highly stressful for the pet and for you.

7. *Pain*

If your pet is sensitive to touch, this is a clear indicator of pain. Another indicator is when you see your pet isolating himself from you and/or shying away from "favorite spots." Inability to move can also be a sign of pain or discomfort. You should immediately take your pet to the veterinarian to assess the situation. Medication is a good option, but you must also consider how long you want your pet to sustain life through artificial means. It is also important to consider any side effects of the pain medication and the effects these will have on your animal's quality of life.

8.   *Treatment Potential*
When your pet falls ill it is only logical to consult a veterinarian. Speak honestly and seriously with your vet to assess the situation and consider all of the factors. Will the proposed treatment be effective? Will it be long lasting? What medications will be required and what are the side effects? You should also consider the stress that the pet will be under during its treatment and visits to the vet.

You are the best judge of your pet's quality of life and it is important for you to assess the situation honestly. To accomplish this, you need to be aware of your needs and those of your pet.

18. Final Decisions: Hospice and Euthanasia

With Andy, events at the end happened way too quickly. He got progressively worse and was in so much obvious pain at the end that he couldn't even walk. He would go to the bathroom right where he lay. He was also blind.

Even then, I was in denial and still trying to bargain my way out of this situation. I didn't know that when I took him to the vet that morning, it would be the last time I would ever see him. I first realized something was wrong when the vet left me alone in a room with Andy, with delicious dog treats. The vet then told me to say my final good-byes to him.

Even though I'd always been careful not to overfeed Andy, all bets were off now. I gave him all he could eat and he loved it! I told him again and again how much I loved him and how he was the best friend I'd ever had.

For the first time in days, Andy wagged his tail. He cuddled with me hard as he said his own goodbye to me. I couldn't believe how placid and how content he was.

When the veterinary staff came to get him, Andy gazed at me one last time, with love in his eyes. Even though I was around a crowd and I hate showing emotion in front of people, I cried uncontrollably. The staff took him away and put him to sleep.

If there's one thing I still struggle with guilt over, it is the fact that I did not go with him when the staff took him away. I'd give anything right now to go back in time and be with my baby in his final moments, when he needed me the most.

I'm thankful, though, that I have his ashes. I have a little altar in my office with his urn on it. Even though I miss him, this really helped me transition to the acceptance stage. The altar and ashes enable me to honor his memory and to have him with me throughout each day.

Looking back on the ordeal, one more thing I want to point out is how much it helped to give Andy pain killers. It kept him alive longer so that the two of us could enjoy each other and be together in happiness. What I found interesting was that Andy was great at living in the present moment. He didn't dread the future which taught me that neither should I.

Though his quality of life blipped upward temporarily, the cancer caught up with him slowly but surely. Gradually, the pain became too much for even the pain medication to handle. I had to realize that keeping him alive was now inhumane.

Once you make a serious assessment of your pet's quality of life, you can begin to consider your options. Two likely alternatives are hospice care and euthanasia. While it's difficult to think of your pet's final moments, it's important to make decisions about the situation as soon as possible. Consult your pet's veterinarian and the rest of your family to do the best you can for your beloved pet.

Hospice Care

Hospice is a familiar program for humans, but in 2001 the American Veterinary Medical Association approved guidelines for hospice care for animals. Though it's not widely available at the present time, there will likely be an increase in availability.

Hospice care is a way to allow humans, and now animals, to die with dignity. In cases of terminally ill patients who have exhausted all treatment possibilities, hospice care provides relief from pain and the chance to pass on quietly and painlessly in the company of those they love rather than a more chaotic medical environment.

Hospice care gives the family time to say goodbye to their beloved animal and at the same time provides tangible benefits to the pet.

Benefits to Pets

- ✓ Comfort
- ✓ One-on-one time with the people they love
- ✓ Favorite foods and treats
- ✓ A sense of calm and safety

If you elect to provide hospice care for your pet, you need to understand fully what it will entail in your situation. It is crucial to have good communication with your veterinarian and to have a complete understanding of your pet's condition. You will be ultimately responsible for the care of your pet, and you need to commit to it from the start.

At the same time, you must also be aware of your limits and of those of your pet.

What steps do I take?

1. *Contact your veterinarian to assess the situation.*

   This should be the first thing that you do once you have been made aware of your pet's chronic or terminal illness. Ask the vet's professional opinion about the animal's comfort and life expectancy. You will also want to ask specific questions about medication, frequency of dosage, visits to the vet, what to do about worsening conditions, and the cost. Don't be afraid to ask your vet for help in making the decision. Veterinarians are very familiar with all of the issues at hand and can help share the burden.

2. *Do your own research about the condition.*

   Talking to the vet is the first step, but there's also a wealth of information available to you. Do a simple Internet search on your pet's condition or seek out a forum of other pet owners who may have dealt with a similar situation. (See http://www.petlossguide.com/resources for some helpful sites.) Getting input from those who have experienced the hospice situation firsthand can be very helpful and will provide information that cannot be gained from a book or veterinarian.

3. *Assess if this is really for you or for your pet.*

   Be honest with yourself about your reasons for choosing hospice care. Is it about your desire to keep the animal with you as long as possible OR is it about your pet's quality of life and comfort? This is a difficult question to answer and to answer honestly, but it must be done.

4. *Get input from the rest of your family.*

   This is not a decision to be made alone. Consult the others you love and who love your pet.

5. *Decide if you are physically and financially able to take on this type of care.*
   Hospice care for pets is a serious undertaking. You may not be able to leave your pet alone, and you may need to invest in expensive medications. You also need to consider the physical aspects. If you have a 100 pound dog, you may not be able to provide appropriate care if he or she has mobility issues. Talk all of these things over with both your vet and your family to best assess the situation.

6. *Ask yourself if you are psychologically prepared to watch your pet die.*
   You may not want to say goodbye to your pet, but you also need to consider how difficult it will be to watch your pet die. Your pet may quickly become an animal

you don't know, especially if in pain. You also want to think about how you want to remember your pet. Watching an animal slowly deteriorate may make it difficult to remember the good times that you spent together.

7.   *Know what the limits are for you and your pet.*
Know when you or your pet has had enough. This is a difficult situation for all those involved and you need to respect the physical and psychological limits. Saying goodbye does not make you a bad pet owner. The animal that brought you happiness for so long would not want to suffer or to make you suffer.

Euthanasia

The word euthanasia comes from the Greek word to mean "fortunate or happy in death." Euthanasia is a compassionate way of ending the life of an animal suffering from a chronic or terminal illness. While this is a controversial concept with respect to humans, there is little question about its use with animals.

Conflicts that people may have with euthanasia are that it is artificially ending a life or that it is a selfish act. There couldn't be anything further from the truth. If you're dealing with a terminally ill animal, what you are deciding is when to stop artificially forcing the animal to live. And believe me nothing is more selfish than prolonging the life of an animal in pain. Euthanasia is not an easy decision to arrive at, but there may come a certain point when it becomes the only compassionate choice.

Find others who have had to make a similar decision. Talk it over with them to find out what they now feel about it. You're the one who will ultimately make the decision, but it's nice to get input from others with experience.

How to prepare

Once you've decided to euthanize your pet, you'll want to take that extra time to say goodbye. Go to your pet's favorite park. Let your pet play with his favorite toy. Buy your pet her favorite treats. Let your pet sleep on the furniture! And most importantly, remember all of the good times you've had together and try to spend whatever time is left together. Some people feel that their pets let them know when it is time to go, and if you have that connection with your pet, respect what you think your pet's wishes are.

What's going to happen?

1.   *Talk to your vet.*

When making such an important decision you should talk to your veterinarian to fully understand the procedure. Ask as many questions as you need. Some people find it comforting to know exactly what will happen from the medical perspective, while others don't want to know. Do what is best for you.

2.   *Decide what to do with the body.*

This may seem morbid, but it's a good idea to make this decision before you're at the veterinarian's office. Refer to the following section to look at some options. You'll also want to think about the memorial service, if you plan to have one. If you elect to hold a more formal service and burial, contact the local pet cemetery ahead of time.

3.   *Spend time with your pet and prepare your family for the final goodbye.*

You're probably spending significantly more time with your pet and spoiling your pet since you've made the decision. Know that you're doing what is best for your beloved companion and that he or she loves you unconditionally. Your pet doesn't see you in a negative way; your pet expects you to do what is best.

4.   *Love your pet and don't feel guilty.*

The day you take your pet to be euthanized will be a very difficult one. Remember that your calmness and relaxed manner will ease the anxiety of your pet. Talk to your pet as she goes to sleep and remember that she knows you love her. Take time with your pet after the procedure and say your final goodbye.

Journaling Questions: Final Decisions

When faced with an ill pet, you may need to make decisions about the end of the pet's life. Use these questions to guide your decision-making process.

What is the pet's condition and is there a chance for a cure?

_____

_____

_____

_____

_____

What are the pros and cons of providing hospice care for your pet?

_____

_____

_____

_____

_____

_____

_____

_____

_____

_____

Why do you want to provide hospice care?

_____

_____

_____

_____

_____

_____

_____

_____

_____

_____

_____

What are the pros and cons of euthanizing your pet?

_____

_____

_____

_____

_____

_____

_____

_____

How do you feel about euthanasia?

_____

_____

_____

_____

_____

_____

_____

_____

_____

_____

_____

What would your pet want?

_____

_____

_____

_____

_____

_____

_____

_____

_____

19. Handling the Remains

Deciding what to do with the remains of your pet is an unpleasant yet necessary task. There are a variety of options and as is the case for every step of this process, you must do what is best for you, your pet, and your family.

It's also important to do research on the services available in your area. Discuss your options with your pet's veterinarian as the vet is probably aware of the possibilities in your town and may be able to provide you with contact information to get you started.

What are my options?

> *Cremation*
>
> *Pet Cemetery Burial*
>
> *At-home Burial*
>
> *Pet Preservation*
>
> *Disposal*

1.   *Cremation*

I have always gotten my pets cremated so that (as I see it) they will be with me always. Cremation is a common method to dispose of a body and can be done in one of two ways: personal or group cremation.

Personal cremations allow for your pet to be cremated alone and for you to receive your pet's cremains at the end of the process. You can provide an urn or container in which to keep the cremains and you can either keep or bury the cremains. While processes vary from place to place, it is typically possible to arrange for the body to be moved without you having to take on this duty.

Group cremations, on the other hand, are ideal for those pet owners who have no need to have the cremains returned to them. Your pet is cremated with other deceased animals and then the crematorium disposes of their cremains, typically by spreading them in a pasture or other appropriate area. This is typically less expensive and no less respectful of your pet's life.

2.   *Pet Cemetery Burial*

Pet cemeteries provide similar services to those of human cemeteries and sometimes even more. This is a good way to find an eternal resting place for your beloved pet. The laws governing pet cemeteries vary from place to place, so it will be important to research the laws appropriate to your area. You will want to find out if there is a deed restriction on the land that will ensure that the pet cemetery remains a pet cemetery and is not otherwise developed in the future.

It's also possible to invest in above-ground mausoleums that are easily moved if there is no deed restriction or if you move. In this way, you can be sure to always know where your companion rests. Small services can typically be arranged, and the directors of pet cemeteries are good resources for dealing with both the technical and emotional details of a pet's death.

3.   *At-home Burial*

Some people choose to bury either the ashes or the bodies of their pets at home. It's important to research the laws in your area as it is illegal in some places to dispose of pet remains in this way. You can inquire at the public health department to learn the rules in your town. This is an inexpensive option, though you also must consider that you can't take your pet with you if you move. Should you move, the fate of your pet's gravesite will be in the hands of the new homeowners. And they may not appreciate having a burial site in their yard.

4.   *Pet Preservation*

A controversial option presents itself in the form of pet preservation. Different from taxidermy, pet preservation is a process in which a pet can be preserved through a freeze-drying process. There are increasing numbers of companies that specialize in this process and it is worth investigating if it appeals to you. This process can be costly and take months to complete, but may be worth it to you if the notion of always having your companion animal by your side appeals to you.

Unlike taxidermy, the freeze-drying process allows for your pet to be positioned in the particular pose you specify. Many people find this option morbid, but most of those who choose to preserve their pet in this way are happy with the results. Again, it's important to thoroughly research the company you plan to work with in order to avoid disingenuous people who do not respect the life of your pet.

5.   *Clinical Disposal*

This need not be as cold as it sounds. Veterinarians are well-equipped to dispose of the bodies, typically for a fee that is based on the size of the animal. You should discuss this with your veterinarian when assessing your options. Be sure to ask the vet about his or her disposal methods so that you are comfortable with the final moments of your pet's physical existence.

Watch out though. In many cases, pets are accumulated and then disposed of en masse, sometimes either to a rendering facility of sorts or to a garbage dump. To be as fair as possible, a positive spin to rendering is that your pet's body is being recycled into the chain of life. However, if you don't feel comfortable with this, investigate this option thoroughly before choosing it to be sure that you're dealing with reputable organizations. It's important for you to do what feels best for YOU. Remember, the lifeless body is no longer your beloved companion, but his or her spirit will live on through you.

A final word about veterinary disposal – I have talked to many people who have pursued this option and then felt guilty later on. Do not allow yourself to think this way. Your baby's body is just an empty shell that remains behind while the soul goes away to a better place.

Whatever you choose to do with the remains of your pet, remember that your pet will live forever through your heart. Your pet exists not through its remains, but through the warm sun you feel on your skin, through the air you breathe, and through the breeze you hear by the sea. Your pet is everywhere with you because he or she lives on in your memories.

As long as you cherish and hold onto your love for your pet, your pet is still with you. There is nothing separating the two of you except for the passage of time. Remember the good times and how much you loved your pet.

Once you have made the decision about what to do with the body, move forward with a focus on a memorial. Memorials can be formal or informal, private or public. Choose something that respects both your and your pet's wishes, desires, and preferences.

20. Funerary Services

When a pet dies, the handling of the memorial service is not straightforward. There's an entire range of possibilities from doing nothing at all to a full service and burial. In this section, I will provide some options that you may want to consider. Also, check for resources available in your area that could provide additional support. The most important thing to remember during this process is to listen to your heart. You need to do what is right for you, your pet, and your family.

What are the options?

No service

Private at-home "non-service"

At-home service

Pet friendly service and reception

Formal service and burial

1. *No service*

   Having a service of any kind is not mandatory, though many people find it to be comforting. Lack of a service does not mean a lack of love for your pet. Being alone with your thoughts may be exactly what you need. A private moment, just for you, will help you to say goodbye in a positive way.

2. *Private at-home "non-service"*

   Whether you live alone or have a partner or family, you may elect to take a moment to think of your beloved pet when you are all together. This could be as you gather your pet's belongings for donation or disposal, or even spontaneously as a memory comes to mind. You can think of your dog, cat, guinea pig, or other pet during happier times. Think about when and how you enjoyed spending time with them the most.

The best part of a "non-service" is that it can happen any time the mood strikes. Perhaps after a meal you and your dining partner(s) might share a story about the deceased, such as "Remember how Harry used to love to clean the plates after dinner?" There is no specific format or length; this is just impromptu memory sharing amongst those who love the deceased most.

3.   *At-home service*

It may be important for you and your family to do more than spend a quiet moment remembering your pet. You may want to organize a small service within the family or close circle of friends where you can all share memories of the deceased. Find a picture of your pet and have those involved tell their favorite stories of time spent with the animal.

If children are involved, you could spend some time talking about death and what it means. For children, saying goodbye to a pet is complicated. If this is the case, you could set up a memorial craft project of sorts so that children have the opportunity to express themselves in a number of ways. Some examples include collage making, drawing, painting or coloring. Or, as a group you could all create a pictorial memorial that could be hung or placed in the home. The service does not have to be formal, and you're free to structure it any way you like.

4.   *Pet friendly service and reception*

This is a great option for those pet owners who not only had a connection with their pet, but with a group of animals as well. Perhaps you and your pet always visited a particular animal park or belonged to an animal-centric club.

Organizing a pet friendly service and reception is an effective way to include your pet's friends and your friends when saying a final goodbye to the deceased. This can be as formal or informal as you wish; the main issue is that you remember your pet. You can set up a treat bar for the visiting animals and refreshments for your human guests.

Have a guest book for visitors to sign and post pictures of your pet. For those who want to contribute in some way, you can provide information on donation possibilities. Again, you can organize a special service or just run the function as a reception. Do what's best for you!

5.   *Formal service and burial*

If you choose a burial for your pet, it's likely that you can arrange a formal service through the pet cemetery you have chosen. They'll probably have a standard service that they provide which can be personalized to your needs. In addition to the graveside service, you may also want to host a reception in your home similar to the reception described above.

Choosing a way to memorialize your pet can be an overwhelming but rewarding process. If you elect not to have a ceremony, you could consider an alternative memorial.

21. Alternative Memorials

In addition to a service, there are many other ways in which you can memorialize your pet. It's important to remember your pet, but it is equally important not to become obsessed with the deceased. Creating an appropriate memorial can be your opportunity to be creative and express your feelings.

For some, creating the final memorial marks closure to the death of the loved one. Memorials are meant to celebrate the life of a loved one. There are some excellent possibilities that embrace life in an active way and enable you to remember your loved one at the same time.

Personal Possibilities

The loss of a pet is personal and you may want to memorialize in private. The following options center on things you can do at home or by yourself to create a memorial.

Plant a tree, bush, or plant
Choose a spot in your yard that your pet particularly loved, if an outdoor pet, or a place special to you, if an indoor pet and plant something. This plant can then be a constant reminder of life and regeneration. You may also want to place a marker with your pet's name on it in the area you've chosen. If you don't have a yard, buy yourself a houseplant or an indoor tree. A Bonsai tree is a great option because it requires a certain amount of attention.

Scatter ashes in a special spot
You may not want to hold onto the cremains after you've had your service (formal or informal). If not, you can take the ashes to a special place and scatter them. You can elect to do this in your yard or another place where you feel particularly close to your pet. Did you take a perfect vacation with your pet? Is there a trail that you often walked together? The most important thing is to do something that is significant to you.

Find a special place for cremains
If you elect to keep your pet's cremains, you'll want to find a meaningful place for them. You could keep them indoors on a mantle or shelf or create a special area in the yard.

Engrave a stone or plaque
A marker of sorts is a nice way to incorporate your beloved pet into your everyday world. Stones are particularly appropriate for a garden marker, and a plaque can be placed anywhere. You could even engrave a meaningful phrase or poem to commemorate your pet.

Make a photo collage
One of the most common methods of memorializing is the photo collage. Retail stores offer many styles of collage frames, and with this option you can really be creative. For example, you could buy a number of matching frames for a table display. Alternatively, you could create a wall display or a freestanding photo screen. Be sure to include photos of you and your family with your pet so that the display is not just about death but embraces life as well.

Create a scrapbook
Scrapbooking is a great project for any age. Many products are available to help you create a scrapbook that's truly unique and original. Creating a smaller scrapbook that's devoted only to your pet is very therapeutic. Scrapbooking is also a great activity for children. This, like many of these options, can be an on-going project that can be added to and updated as time goes on.

Commission a portrait or sculpture
Many artists can create beautiful works of art from a good photograph of your pet. This is a nice extra option that you can hold onto for a long time.

Purchase a memorial item
Shopping therapy can be beneficial. Maybe you'll find the perfect item that captures your pet's personality or life. It could be anything! You don't need to restrict yourself to traditional funerary items like plaques or grave markers. If you are a cat lover, look for an artistic feline item. If you love fish, invest in a new aquatic shower curtain. The possibilities are endless!

Write something
Writing is the best way to collect and process your thoughts. If you haven't already started filling out the questions in this book, now is the time.

Create a charm bracelet
If your interest lies in jewelry, this is a nice way to commemorate your beloved pet. You can purchase charms in the shape of your pet and of things that remind you of the pet. You can add to the bracelet yearly or on special occasions. This is also a great gift to give to a child who may have lost a pet.

Take Action!

In addition to affecting your life, your pet's death can help to spur positive change for other animals and humans alike. These options encourage you to become active in the world and to involve yourself with other animals and animal lovers. There are many other options available. Just take time to research your opportunities!

Send memory cards
Use your creative side to make announcements to send to your friends and relatives. You could write a short tribute to your pet and include a picture. If so inclined, include a list of organizations that take donations on behalf of pets.

Post a tribute online
There are a variety of websites dedicated to celebrating animals. Post your pet's story for others to celebrate. Be sure to do your research! You want to be involved with a reputable site. If you must pay to post your tribute, be certain that the monies are going to help animals, not into the pockets of the greedy.

Create a memorial web page
These days the world is on the Internet! Take this opportunity and run with it. It is very easy to create your own tribute web site that can educate others about your beloved friend and provide information that can help others. Use this space to make a difference and to help others get involved with animals. You can also provide discussion space for other grievers or post information that you think others need to know.

Involve yourself in animal rights
So many animals needlessly suffer every day and that misfortune gives you a tremendous opportunity to get involved! A great resource is http://animalconcerns.org This website provides great links to information about ways you can help.

Donate money to help animals
There are many organizations that work to help and protect animals locally, nationally, and internationally. Research organizations in your area or donate to one of the organizations below:

American Society for the Prevention of Cruelty to Animals: http://www.aspca.org

Humane Society of the United States: http://www.hsus.org/

National Humane Education Society: http://www.nhes.org/

World Wildlife Federation: http://worldwildlife.org

The Living Planet Campaign: http://www.livingplanet.org

National Wildlife Federation: http://www.nwf.org

The Nature Conservancy: http://www.tnc.org

People for the Ethical Treatment of Animals: http://www.peta.org

Spay USA: http://www.spayusa.org

PLEASE NOTE: Though all of the organizations listed above help animals, some may have practices that conflict with your beliefs. For example, you may not agree with the strict moral views of PETA, or you may have issues with some of The Nature Conservancy's wildlife population control practices. That's why it's important to research the groups first to find out those that most fit your values.

Establish a fund
Do you live near a veterinary school or other animal-related training facility? You could establish scholarships for students who choose to spend their lives devoted to animals.

Contribute to a cure
If your pet died of a particular disease, another option is to give money towards finding a cure. Check with your veterinarian or conduct independent research on how this can best be done. You might not have been able to help your pet, but you may be able to make a difference in the life of another animal.

"Adopt" a zoo animal
Many zoos offer the chance to "adopt" an animal. In this type of arrangement, the money you donate can go directly towards the care of a particular zoo animal. Check with your local zoo to see if it has programs such as this or other programs in which you can participate.

Donate items needed at local animal shelters
Often animal shelters are in need of more than just money. Many are looking for donations of blankets, leashes, pet toys, cleaning supplies, food, and other pet-related items. Contact your local animal shelter and ask for a copy of its donation list.

Volunteer at an animal shelter or other animal organization
Animal shelters and organizations are always in need of caring volunteers. Volunteers can help in many ways including spending time with the animals, helping to bathe them, or staffing an adoption or other type of event. Very often, the ability to contribute time is more important than contributing money. Contact your local shelter for more information.

Learn about pet therapy
Pets have a healing and comforting affect on many people. Learn more about the possibility of sharing the love of animals with those who can't have their own pets. A great resource is http://www.deltasociety.org

Become a foster pet caretaker
Many no-kill shelters often need help housing their animals until they can be permanently adopted. This little-known possibility to help animals is the best way to

reintroduce yourself to the possibility of having a new pet. Look into foster care needs in your area by visiting http://www.PetLossGuide.com/resources

---

The Animals' Savior
By Jim Willis

I looked at all the caged animals in the shelter...
the cast-offs of human society.
I saw in their eyes love and hope, fear and dread,
sadness and betrayal.
And I was angry.
"God," I said, "this is terrible! Why don't you do something?"
God was silent for a moment and then He spoke softly.
"I have done something," He replied.
"I created *you*."

From Pieces of My Heart: Writings Inspired by Animals and Nature by Jim Willis, 1999 (Used With Permission From the Author.)

Organize a benefit event to help animals
Help to create a benefit in your area. Organize a walk-a-thon, car wash, adopt-a-pet or other event to benefit animals in your area. Contact area shelters to see how you can help.

Celebrate National Pet Memorial Day
The International Association of Pet Cemeteries (IAPC) has named the second Sunday in September as National Pet Memorial Day. Pet cemeteries typically observe this day with special events. Visit the IAPC website at http://www.iaopc.com for more information.

Celebrate animals every day
Take time to think of the animals! Respect them in your everyday life and encourage others to do so as well.

22. How to ROAR

It's easy to remain passive during the grief process and to see yourself as nothing more than a helpless victim. For this reason, it's important to use your acceptance of the situation as a jumping off point for a renewed commitment to your life. Going beyond the five stages of grief helps you to ROAR into a new existence. How is this done? As I've mentioned numerous times throughout this book, grief is a difficult process that each person experiences in a different way. But there is one very important element to grieving and that is to remember to live. This is what I mean when I refer to "roaring" back into the world:

R = ***Respect your loss and grief***

O = ***Own your reality***

A = ***Affirm yourself***

R = ***Reclaim your life***

R – Respect your loss and grief

Not only do you need to acknowledge and accept the fact that you have lost something that is very important in your life, you need to respect it too. Your loss is a valid loss whether others believe it to be or not. Respecting the loss means to admit that there has been a loss and that it is legitimate. The death of your cat, dog or hamster does leave a temporarily empty space in your life, one that you should and you need to recognize. This recognition should not govern your life, but accept that it will likely be a significant part of your present life.

O – Own your reality

Owning your reality means that you accept your current circumstances. This does not mean that you aren't "allowed" to have emotional moments or to continue to cherish your deceased pet. You don't have to like the situation to own it. Owning your reality basically means that you are living for the present moment and that you are taking steps to move forward.

At this stage, consider disposing of the items around your home that remind you of your pet. Keep your mementos and your pictures, but it's really not necessary to keep the old stock of food, the leashes and the toys. If they're in a reasonably good condition, consider donating these items to an animal shelter so that you can help other animals in need.

Loss of a pet is similar in many ways to the loss of a human. For one thing, this person or pet cannot be immediately replaced and might never be fully replaced. Additionally, you've got to get used to your life without your companion. What does it mean to live without your cherished companion? Previously I offered several ideas to help you move on. You might consider becoming a foster parent to one or more pets currently being cared for by an animal rescue group. This is actually a good way to reincorporate animals into your family and your world. It also offers two additional benefits: You are helping to save animals and you are beginning to heal the loss that you've experienced.

Many people may not want to take on the responsibility of another pet, and that's okay. There are plenty of other ways to contribute to life. Volunteering to help others in need helps you work towards becoming at peace with your life as it is. Try each day to celebrate the life you lead and the lives of those you love.

A – Affirm yourself

After the loss of a pet, it's important for you to think positively again about life and about yourself. In this stage you will embrace your own greatness and explore the process of self-affirmation. These positive thoughts will counteract the negative thoughts you have been thinking about yourself and your life.

This means you'll take an active part in improving the way you live and the way you think about life. You're giving yourself permission to grow and change and focus on yourself. Letting go of the emotional baggage that has been weighing you down will allow you to realize a better world for yourself.

During this stage of the process, you will want to create a series of affirmations for yourself that will help you to improve your life. Affirmations are positive things you say out loud, every day, and by doing so, you work towards making true the things you say. The best way to understand the power of affirmations is to think about the things you most want to change in your life and start there. I've outlined a few affirmations below, but your affirmations can be anything you believe, as long as it's a positive thought.

Sample Self-Affirmations

- ✓ "I can handle the changes that come to me."

- ✓ "I know what I want out of life."
- ✓ "I can survive this loss."
- ✓ "I deserve to be happy."

R – Reclaim your life

When you reach this stage, embracing life again is such an exciting possibility and you should now be at a point where you are able to do just that. You have acknowledged and dealt with the pain of death. You have explored the grief process and you know how to move on. You respect the lives of those no longer here and appreciate that you need to live joyfully too. Guilt, denial and anger are banished from your outlook, and though you accept the loss and are emotionally healthy once again, you still feel sad sometimes but are also able to focus mostly on the good times you had with your pet. You may have already taken on the joy of a new pet. Congratulations my friend, you have just begun to ROAR!!!

Journaling Questions: Creating Affirmations

When you learn to ROAR you need to learn the art of self-affirmations. Use these pages to start ROARing back into the world.

The first step to constructing your self-affirmations is to think of positive phrases and words that you would like to associate with yourself. Examples could be: survive, strength, alive, happy, relax, etc.

Write a list of words and phrases that describe who you want to be:

_____   _____   _____

_____   _____   _____

_____   _____   _____

_____   _____   _____

_____   _____   _____

_____   _____   _____

_____   _____   _____

—————————— —————————— ——————————

—————————— —————————— ——————————

—————————— —————————— ——————————

Using these words and expressions begin to construct affirmations. Examples could be:

"I will survive this grieving process."

"Each day is a better day."

"My memory of the great times I had with [Pet's Name] gives me strength."

Now, write your own affirmation in each of the squares on the pages that follow and cut out the squares. You may want to laminate the sheets before you cut the cards. Keep these cards where you know you will see them each day and recite an affirmation to yourself throughout the day. You may want to keep these thirty and use the same ones each month, OR you may choose to create new affirmations each month.

Journaling Questions: Your Story

You have gone through a lot during your grieving process. Take these final pages to write the story of your pet. Write it so that it is your pet's life story, or write a fictional account, or write a story from the perspective of your pet. Use this writing time to connect with your pet's memory. Be sure to give it a title.

_____

_____

_____

_____

_____

_____

_____

_____

_____

_____

_____

_____

_____

_____

_____

_____

_____

_____

_____

_____

_____

_____

_____

_____

_____

_____

_____

_____

_____

_____

_____

_____

_____

_____

_____

A Special Bonus For You

Please visit
www.petlossguide.com/resources
for additional information to guide you on your recovery.

**Robin Jean Brown
with her newly
adopted dog,
Joesy.**

Writing this book helped me work through a difficult time in my life. I hope that reading this book and working through the Journaling Questions has helped you too.

Wishing You Peace,

Robin Jean Brown

Printed in the United Kingdom
by Lightning Source UK Ltd.
134469UK00001B/1/A